Mike and Harriet McManus are playing
ica. They have teamed up with more tl
Community Marriage Policies. An independent study reports that in their first 122 communities, divorce rates fell 17.5 percent in seven years, with some plunging 50 percent, cohabitation rates dropped by a third, and marriage rates are rising as a result of the Community Marriage Policies. Mike and Harriet are not only passionate, they are effective. I highly recommend you join with them in the mission to restore marriage in America.

—Tony Perkins, president, Family Research Council

In this groundbreaking book, Mike and Harriet McManus dispel the myth that living together before marriage leads to "happy ever after" and give the secrets for making marriages succeed. No one is more qualified to help couples prepare for marriage. Based on their years of training over 4,000 Mentor Couples and their personal, 97 percent marriage-saving success rate in their own church, Mike and Harriet offer couples marriage insurance no one should ever live without!

—Claudia & David Arp, founders, 10 Great Dates, and
authors of *10 Great Dates Before You Say "I Do"*

For too long, church leaders have ignored cohabitation. This book is a wake-up call on the extent of the problem—with encouraging, proven answers. It is must-reading for every pastor and lay leader.

—Reverend Richard Cizik, vice president of the National Association of Evangelicals

Mike and Harriet McManus are doing their level best to alert Americans to the fact that cohabitation increases rather than decreases the likelihood of divorce. The authors, who have devoted their lives to the cause of marriage, have written a well-researched and practical book. It deserves close attention by young people, their parents, and by the Church, which has been largely silent on the matter. *Living Together* provides youth with the insights and tools needed to avoid what could be one of the costliest mistakes of their lives and shows them the path to a happy and lasting marriage.

—George H. Gallup, Jr., founding chairman of the Gallup International Institute

The message is clear—living together is not a good way to prepare for marriage. Mike and Harriet McManus reveal the common myths about cohabitation that couples use to justify their decision. Premarital preparation can create stronger marriages, and these programs include four key components: 1) a premarital inventory, 2) couple mentoring, 3) skill building on communication and conflict resolution, and 4) a strong spiritual relationship. To promote strong marriages, every community needs a Community Marriage Policy like they have championed. This book is a great resource for clergy, marriage educators, and all who want to help build stronger marriages.

—David H. Olson, Ph.D., founder of PREPARE/ENRICH,
president of Life Innovations

Other books by Michael J. McManus

Marriage Savers: Helping Your Friends and Family Avoid Divorce

50 Practical Ways to Take Our Kids Back from the World

Insuring Marriage: 25 Proven Ways to Prevent Divorce

LIVING TOGETHER

MYTHS, RISKS & ANSWERS

MIKE AND HARRIET MCMANUS
FOREWORD BY CHUCK COLSON

HOWARD BOOKS
A DIVISION OF SIMON & SCHUSTER
New York   London   Toronto   Sydney

Our purpose at Howard Books is to:
• *Increase faith* in the hearts of growing Christians
• *Inspire holiness* in the lives of believers
• *Instill hope* in the hearts of struggling people everywhere
Because He's coming again!

HOWARD
BOOKS

Published by Howard Books, a division of Simon & Schuster, Inc.
1230 Avenue of the Americas, New York, NY 10020
www.howardpublishing.com

Living Together © 2008 Michael J. McManus and Harriet E. McManus

Library of Congress Cataloging-in-Publication Data

McManus, Michael J.
Living together : myths, risks & answers / Mike and Harriet McManus.
p.   cm.
ISBN-13: 978-1-4767-0973-4

1. Unmarried couples—Religious aspects—Christianity.   I. McManus, Harriet.   II. Title.
BT705.9.M36   2008
241'.66—dc22   2007038956

10   9   8   7   6   5   4   3   2   1

Manufactured in the United States of America

For information regarding special discounts for bulk purchases,
please contact: Simon & Schuster Special Sales at
1-800-456-6798 or business@simonandschuster.com.

Edited by Between the Lines

Cover design by LUCAS Art & Design, Jenison, MI
Interior design by Davina Mock-Maniscalco
Cover photo by Veer Images; author photo by Melissa McManus

Some of the names used in this book have been changed to
protect the privacy of those who so graciously shared their stories.

We dedicate *Living Together: Myths, Risks & Answers* to couples in healthy marriages who can be found in any church, who might be inspired to serve as a Mentor Couple to help other couples prepare for, enrich, or restore a marriage. We dedicate it to America's clergy who are flummoxed by couples who are living together, in hope that the answers suggested here will help you better serve these couples.

We also dedicate *Living Together* to the parents of cohabiting children, who have not known what to say to them. Finally, we offer this book to couples who are living together, in hope that you will move apart and prepare for marriage in a better way that gives you a 95 percent chance of success, keeping in mind Saint Paul's admonition to "test everything. Hold on to the good. Avoid every kind of evil" (1 Thessalonians 5:21–22).

Acknowledgments

WRITERS STAND ON the shoulders of those who pioneered intellectual and spiritual territory before them. Harriet and I are grateful to Reverend Everett "Terry" Fullam, rector of Saint Paul's Episcopal Church in Darien, Connecticut, who deepened our Christian faith and inspired me to write my "Ethics & Religion" newspaper column, the research for which led to writing *Living Together: Myths, Risks & Answers*. We want to thank Dr. Barbara Markey and Dr. David Olson who created the FOCCUS and PREPARE premarital inventories, tools we have used to mentor couples. We also appreciate Dr. Robert Norris, senior pastor of our church, Fourth Presbyterian in Bethesda, Maryland, who gave us the opportunity to pioneer training couples in healthy marriages to serve as Mentor Couples. We are especially grateful to Diane Sollee, director of Smart Marriages and the mother of the Marriage Movement, for her unending encouragement and support. We thank scholars who created some of the exercises we use, such as Scott Stanley and colleagues at the University of Denver who fashioned the PREP "Speaker-Listener Technique," and Dr. Lori Gordon who created PAIRS communication exercises. We are grateful to the fifty-seven premarital couples we have mentored who have openly shared their lives with us, particularly "Hector" and "Teresa," a cohabiting couple whose growth is detailed in chapter 9. We are also indebted to 10,000 pastors and priests who created Community Marriage Policies, which adopted the reforms outlined in this book in 220 cities, and to thousands of Mentor Couples in their churches whom we have been privileged to train. Our dream is that *Living Together* will multiply their numbers so that every premarital couple will have the privilege of sharing their relationship with a mature married couple. Finally, Harriet and I are grateful to Denny Boultinghouse, the executive editor of Howard Books, who made a commitment to publish *Living Together: Myths, Risks & Answers,* and to Between the Lines, the editing team who reviewed our manuscript. Its editors, Dawn Brandon and Tammy Bicket, did an excellent of job of pruning and polishing our words.

Contents

Foreword

THE PICTURE IN a recent *Washingtonian* magazine perfectly symbolized a nation with the highest divorce rate in the world. It featured a wedding cake with a bride and groom on top. Lurking behind them were two gloomy, dark-suited figures: Two little lawyers, each one holding a copy of the prenuptial agreement.

"Love is all you need—unless the marriage ends in divorce," wrote *Washingtonian* editor Kim Eisler. "Then a prenuptial agreement is the best defense." He called the prenup "a divorce insurance policy." Well, that's probably true—but wouldn't it be better for couples to have a marriage insurance policy?

This is the goal of my friend Mike McManus, cofounder of Marriage Savers with his wife, Harriet. McManus points out that most weddings take place in churches. This means Christians can become a force for building lifelong marriages. But they will accomplish this only if they realize they themselves have become a marital wrecking ball. For instance, when a cohabiting couple asks a pastor to marry them, instead of turning a blind eye to the living-together arrangement (as many ministers do), pastors should insist that the couple move apart and refrain from sexual relations until they tie the knot. If couples protest—and they will—pastors should explain the facts of life to them: Cohabiting couples are much more likely to divorce than couples who do not cohabit prior to marriage. Living apart until the wedding, while inconvenient, is less painful than a divorce down the road.

But pastors shouldn't wait until cohabiting couples come to them. They need to begin marriage preparation years before the young people in their congregations become engaged. They must help teens discover the dangers of living together, and the lifelong rewards of biblical courtship and marriage.

For instance, many people consider cohabitation a stepping-stone toward a happy marriage—especially women; but more often than not, it isn't. Nearly half of all cohabiting couples break up before a marriage ever takes place. Even when these couples do eventually marry, two-thirds will divorce—which means four out of five of the 5.4 million couples now cohabiting will not enjoy a lasting marriage.

Second, many couples think cohabitation is a way to test a relationship, but "you can't practice permanence," as marriage expert Dr. Barbara Markey says. Without a public, lifelong commitment, couples tend to break up at the first sign of trouble.

Third, becoming sexually involved can make a couple feel closer than they actually are, driving them to a marriage based on (temporary) infatuation.

Then there are the health benefits of marriage. Cohabiting couples suffer much higher rates of depression than the married. Women are far more likely to be abused by a live-in boyfriend than a husband. And when cohabiting couples marry, they suffer higher rates of infidelity than those who did not live together before taking their vows.

Tragically, cohabitation harms children, too: A child is far more likely to be abused or even killed by a mother's live-in boyfriend than he or she is by his or her own father. The children born to unmarried couples are at much greater risk of being expelled from school and having a baby out of wedlock, and are twenty times more likely to end up in prison.

Marriage offers financial benefits: By the time they retire, married couples have three to four times the assets as cohabiting couples. The nonpermanent nature of cohabitation makes many couples fearful of pooling their funds.

These are sobering statistics. If we fail to transmit them to the teenagers in our own churches, we are doing them a grave disservice.

We are living at a time when the very idea of biblical marriage is under attack. We need to help our young people understand what true marriage is, and why they should "accept no substitutions." And instead of playing defense by offering our sons and daughters "divorce insurance"—a prenuptial agreement—we ought to go on the offensive, offering them "marriage insurance" instead.

Reading *Living Together: Myths, Risks & Answers* is a great place to start. Mike and Harriet McManus have a proven record: They have prepared hundreds of couples for successful marriage and have taught other Mentor Couples around the country to do the same. Their book is designed for pastors, parents, and marital mentors who are confronted with couples who think they'll be the glorious exception to the cohabitation statistics.

Read this book, and share it with your friends. If enough of us follow its advice, the church can do much to help the country with the highest divorce rate in the world begin to heal America's divorce epidemic.

Chuck Colson

Introduction

Living Together: Myths, Risks & Answers is the result of years of re-search and successful ministry. Through our work with churches and our founding of Marriage Savers, my wife, Harriet, and I have developed a proven system for helping couples see the dangers of moving in together before marriage and instead move into healthy, reward-ing, long-term marriages.

In our nation, tens of millions of couples cohabit, unaware of the dangers to their relationship, to them as individuals, and to others af-fected by their choices. Harriet and I, and even Marriage Savers, can't reach them all. Only when the church pulls together and steps up to fulfill its rightful role can these couples be reached.

We are speaking to church leaders, yes, but we are also speaking to parents and married couples who are a part of the church and who can play an important role in the effort to rescue couples from the risks they incur by cohabiting.

So this book is designed for "equipping the saints." It's a tool for church leaders, a guide for parents of cohabiting adult children, and a call to couples in successful, long-term marriages who can make a dif-ference by serving as mentors.

A TOOL FOR CHURCH LEADERS

One of our primary goals is to put a tool into the hands of clergy who feel ill-equipped to address the growing number of cohabiting couples who ask to be married. Most seminaries do not adequately prepare students to handle this issue. As a result, many pastors are un-acquainted with how to deal with cohabiting couples—so they avoid the issue, unwittingly contributing to our nation's high divorce rate.

Living Together: Myths, Risks & Answers offers ministers a proven strategy to deal with this issue. It will help equip leaders in churches and synagogues to do a better job preparing couples for—and provid-ing ongoing support for—marriage.

If you are a pastor and have not preached on the subject of cohabi-tation, consider doing so. You may not have many couples in church who live together, but it's likely that several of your middle-aged church members have children who cohabit. These parents often don't know what to say to their own offspring when they sense that what they're doing is dangerous. This book will help you give them the an-swers they need.

The apostle Paul warned against merely telling people "what their itching ears want to hear" (2 Timothy 4:3). Organized religion, our culture's stronghold of moral and spiritual principles, has relinquished its leadership to Hollywood without waging so much as a small skir-mish to protect the well-being of God's first institution, marriage. It's time to reclaim that responsibility and lead couples in finding the bountiful blessings God intends for them through marriage.

A GUIDE FOR PARENTS OF COHABITING ADULT CHILDREN

This book is also for parents of cohabiting children. Such parents often feel uneasy about their children's living arrangements. They are powerless over an adult child no longer living under their roof, reluctant to intrude with unsolicited advice. However, as responsible parents, they need to articulate the danger their adult child is inviting by flouting traditional rules of courtship. Rather than remain mute in the face of a sensitive issue, parents can use the information in this book to address the risks their child is incurring. They can not only give voice to their concern but also point to a proven path so their child and his or her partner can appropriately test their relationship.

Cohabiting is a potential disaster from a parental perspective for three reasons:

1. Their adult child may never marry. Millions of couples live together instead of marrying. The number of never-married Americans soared from 21 million in 1970 to 52 million in 2005. Cohabitation has become a substitute for marriage.
2. Even if their son or daughter does marry the cohabiting partner, their chances of divorce are 75 percent. Grim odds.
3. Of cohabiting couples, 41 percent have children living with them. If the couple breaks up or the ensuing marriage fails, the unmarried parent may move back into his or her parents' home—bringing grandchildren to help raise and financially support.

Parents of cohabitors have good reason to persuade their churches to offer rigorous marriage preparation. Undoubtedly, some of these parents are church leaders themselves and can get their pastor's ear. Parents of young adults have both a self-interest and a larger societal interest in seeing that their churches offer marriage insurance.

If you are a parent, ask your pastor some pertinent questions: Does our church offer premarital preparation? If so, what are its features? Is a premarital inventory required? Are trained Mentor Couples part of the program? How many couples taking marriage preparation decide not to marry? (If it is virtually none or less than 5 percent, your church's program is ineffectual. A rigorous marriage prep program will spark 10 to 20 percent to break up, most of whom will avoid a bad marriage before it begins.) Consider volunteering to become a Mentor Couple to help launch the process of helping young couples prepare for and sustain healthy marriages.

If your adult child is contemplating cohabiting or is living with someone already, don't be afraid to tell him or her, "If you dream of marrying someday, don't move in together," or "Please move out of that cohabiting situation. If your companion is worth it, he or she will continue dating you and will ask you to marry." This book will give you the information you need to talk with your children and make a convincing case against cohabitation.

A CALL TO PROSPECTIVE MENTORS

Our hope is that this book will also inspire couples in healthy, long-term marriages who are active members of their congregations to consider becoming Mentor Couples. You are a great, untapped marriage resource. You are a vital part of the answer to the problem of failing marriages. Successfully married couples have gained precious wisdom that can be passed on to younger couples. By becoming mentors, you can share the keys to your own marital success and how you avoided or overcame "bumps in the road."

Mentor Couples have three great gifts to offer premarital couples:

1. time;
2. love of each other and the Lord; and
3. wisdom gleaned in the marriage with which God has blessed them.

The Gospel of Luke tells us, "The Lord appointed seventy-two others and sent them two by two ahead of him to every town and place where he was about to go. He told them, 'The harvest is plentiful, but the workers are few. Ask the Lord of the harvest, therefore, to send out workers into his harvest field'" (Luke 10:1–2).

Consider this passage of scripture from a new perspective: you and your spouse could go out "two by two" and, where couples are in darkness, bring light.

CHAPTER 1
A Beach Encounter

All a man's ways seem innocent to him, but motives are weighed by the LORD.

Proverbs 16:2

Sex is like a great river that is rich and deep and good as long as it stays within its proper channel. The moment a river overflows its banks, it becomes destructive, and the moment sex overflows its God-given banks, it too becomes destructive. Our task is to define as clearly as possible the boundaries placed upon our sexuality and to do all within our power to direct our sexual responses into that deep, rich current.

Richard Foster, *Money, Sex and Power*

DURING VALENTINE'S DAY week in 2003, my wife, Harriet, and I were in the Bahamas to participate in the signing by clergy of a Community Marriage Policy. Nassau clergy members publicly pledged to adopt strategies to build healthy marriages in their churches. We trained pastors and couples in successful marriages to prepare other couples in their congregations for lifelong marriages, to help enrich existing marriages, and to assist couples in crisis. We had left Washington amid a snowstorm to enjoy warm weather and balmy island breezes in mid-February.

One evening I strolled on the beach to enjoy the sun setting over the ocean and started chatting with a couple. Making small talk, the woman asked, "What kind of work do you do?"

"My wife and I created a ministry called Marriage Savers. We train Mentor Couples to help other couples build marriages for life. Also, we help clergy to cut their community's divorce rate by twenty to fifty percent."

"What would you say is the number one reason marriages break up?" she asked, her interest increasing.

"Poor communication—particularly the inability to resolve conflict—is the top issue," I replied. My source was a Gallup Poll of divorced people. It revealed that only 5 percent of marriages break up because of physical abuse, 17 percent due to adultery, and 16 percent because of substance abuse. However, 57 percent of couples attributed their divorce to "incompatibility" or arguments over money, family, or children. Curiously, couples married each other believing they communicated well.

Most people lack communication skills—which can be taught. Oddly, churches and synagogues, which perform 86 percent of weddings, do little to prepare couples for lifelong marriage, such as teaching the skills of listening and problem solving.

That evening in the Bahamas the woman elaborated: "I've been married before, but it didn't work out. He wasn't really my soul mate, like my friend here. We're very happy."

It was dusk, and I couldn't see whether she was wearing a wedding ring, so I asked, "Are you married?"

"No. We're living together. We're in a committed relationship."

I debated for a moment whether I should be candid about the dangers they were courting. Offering unsolicited advice would be considered rude. Yet the couple was playing with fire. They deserved to have some information on the risks of cohabitation. So I said, "Well, couples who marry after living together are fifty percent more likely to divorce than those who remain apart before the wedding."

"We're in the other fifty percent," her partner laughingly responded. "We're not worried by your numbers."

"Everyone in your situation says that. Why do you think you're exempt?"

The woman appeared concerned and asked, "What's wrong with living together?"

"Couples who cohabit create problems that those who live apart don't experience. For instance, do you argue over finances? Most cohabiting couples have heated disputes over 'your money' versus 'my money' and how much each person should contribute toward household expenses."

Her partner nodded in agreement. "That's partly correct."

The woman quickly interjected, "It's not much of a problem. We have a house, and it's wonderful."

I decided to elaborate on why living together is so risky. "There's also more infidelity in cohabiting relationships than among married couples. People who are living together haven't fully committed to one another. Many regard cohabitation as another form of dating and consider themselves still single and available."

Ignoring that information, the man harrumphed, "Well, I think it makes sense to try on the shoe before you buy it."

"That seems reasonable, but it isn't," I countered. "You can't practice permanence. Marriage requires full commitment. It's not like a shoe. The only committed relationship is marriage."

He replied emphatically, "Well, I would never think of marrying someone with whom I hadn't lived. That's the only way to decide."

His partner tactfully tried to change the subject. "How long have you been married?" she asked.

"Thirty-seven years, and we lived apart until we married. This is a time-proven formula for success. Your moving apart would increase your odds for success."

She added. "This will be a second marriage for me, but his first. We've lived together for a year now. Perhaps we should have dinner with you to talk more about these things."

"Are you engaged?"

"No, but it is Valentine's weekend!" she said with a knowing smile.

I sighed. "I hate to be the bearer of bad news, but the longer one cohabits, the greater the danger of a future divorce. It's less of a problem if a couple lives together two months before the wedding. But you're now a year into it, and he has made no commitment. That's typical of a lot of men. Many men cohabit with partner A, then move on to B, then C, then D. They can always find another willing live-in partner. Women's window of opportunity—based on youth, beauty, and childbearing ability—is much shorter. They waste precious time cohabiting."

The man sat morosely, staring out at the calm blue sea in silence. The woman shut down as well. I excused myself and walked inside to join Harriet for dinner. Despite the woman's comment that they might join us, the couple did not appear in the hotel dining room. Harriet was not surprised. "They're probably having a big argument right now," she said. "You've put words to her fears, and now she's asking him whether he's going to marry her. We won't see them for dinner."

She was right: we didn't see them at dinner or any other time during our stay at the small hotel.

Like the couple on the beach that day, tens of millions of Americans have bought into the myth that living together before marriage will lead to happily ever after . . . and they end up walking away from each other and from marriage itself.

Though the woman's previous marriage had failed—which should have made her cautious—she clearly believed that living together was a step toward marriage. She hoped her partner might propose on Valentine's Day weekend. She said of her beloved, "We're soul mates."

12 Myths About Cohabitation

Cohabitors as a group believe key myths, and these misconceptions encourage them to live together. Following are some common myths along with brief refutations.

- "Everyone's doing it." *No, nearly half of couples are not.*
- "Living together is a step toward marriage." *No, it is a step toward breakup—either before or after the wedding.*
- "We are in a committed relationship." *Untrue. The only truly committed relationship is marriage.*
- "Living together is a trial marriage." *Actually, cohabitation is the worst possible preparation for a healthy marriage. It increases the odds of divorce by 50 percent.*
- "We can't afford to move apart." *Singles can save just as much money by living with someone of the same gender.*
- "We love each other, so it's okay." *If you really loved each other, you would do what's best for each other and for the relationship—what's sanctioned by God and proven through the ages to be the safest, best, most fulfilling way to love.*
- "It can't hurt anybody." *At least one partner is hurt if the relationship disintegrates, which it is likely to do. Also, since cohabitors are as likely as married couples to have children, if the relationship ends, the children feel abandoned and experience significant trauma that can have lifelong effects.*
- "A marriage license is just a piece of paper." *No, it represents a way of life, a state of being blessed by God and sanctioned by the church, government, and community. It affects*

(continued)

every aspect of life: health, happiness, longevity, and sex. They're all better with that "piece of paper."

- "We're getting married anyway." *Don't be so sure. Half of couples living together do not marry—and those who do are much more likely to divorce. Even a month's cohabitation damages the relationship.*

- "What we do is no one's business." *Cohabitation is everyone's business. It threatens society morally and burdens it financially. Eight out of ten cohabiting relationships will fail before or after the wedding, which costs taxpayers a staggering $185 billion a year.*

- "The Bible doesn't mention cohabitation." *Jesus confronted the woman at the well, saying, "You have had five husbands, and you aren't even married to the man you're living with now" (John 4:18, NLT). It was a gentle rebuke, but she was convicted, telling others, "Come and see a man who told me everything I ever did" (John 4:29, NLT).*

- "Cohabitation, marriage, and divorce are simply different lifestyle choices." *"This is the most powerful and dangerous myth," write Linda Waite and Maggie Gallagher in* The Case for Marriage. *"Marriage is not only a private vow, it is a public act, a contract, taken in full public view, enforceable by law and in the equally powerful court of public opinion."*

Really? If so, after a year of living together, why had he still not asked her to marry him? Clearly, he didn't want to. At first blush, the relationship seemed as joyous as that of newlyweds. An hour later, she seemed shaken, and declined to join us for dinner to become better informed—which had been her idea.

Imagine how that woman on the beach will feel when her "soul mate" says, "I love you, but I'm not ready to get married." Does she give him another year to decide? Perhaps, but the only thing that's certain is that she will be a year older and likely still unmarried.

What has living together done to her? Made her bitter? Stolen her time? Trashed her self-confidence? She'll likely experience a "premarital divorce" every bit as painful as a real divorce. And she might never recover her share of the money she invested in the house they bought together: unlike a spouse, she has no legal protection as a cohabiting partner.

Will she attract another man to marry her? Perhaps not. The number of never-married men and women rose from 21 million in 1970 to 52 million by 2005. Why?

Every year millions of men and women, in annually increasing numbers, move in together. Some men allege that they want to "test the relationship." He might explain that he wants to "make sure we're compatible." His girlfriend reads this as a prelude to engagement. She perceives this step as an audition for marriage—an opportunity to show him what a great companion she is. She deludes herself that she is in a "trial marriage."

Typically, women are far more committed than men. In fact, many men who begin living with a woman have no intention of marrying her, despite what they may say about "testing the relationship."

" 'Will you walk into my parlor?' said the spider to the fly."[1] From the fly's perspective, the consequences are likely to be the sort of evil Paul counseled us to avoid: "Test everything. Hold onto the good. Avoid every kind of evil" (1 Thessalonians 5:21–22). With a cohabitation failure rate of 80 percent—before or after the wedding—a couple who decides to live together *is* choosing evil.

A woman frequently senses before a man that she has met a potential life mate. If he asks her to move in with him, she often will agree in hopes of sparking a proposal. Or she may suggest that they live together, believing it to be a step toward securing a future husband. The male's motivation to cohabit is radically different from a woman's. He would rather live with a woman than live alone. Why not? She can pick up some of his living expenses, cook his meals, wash his clothes, and be a handy sex partner. He can have the benefits of marriage without any of the responsibilities.

A man knows the odds are good that if he asks her to marry him, she will do so. Of that there is little doubt. Most men who begin to live with a woman are nowhere close to popping the question. A man doesn't need to live with a woman first to know if she would be a suitable mate. For thousands of years men and woman have successfully bonded without cohabiting first.

The percentage of never-married Americans aged thirty to forty-four more than tripled from only 6.8 percent in 1970 to 20.4 percent in 2003—and there's a reason. Tens of millions of women are agreeing to live in unwed relationships with men—and are losing their opportunity to marry. In today's sex-saturated culture, where cohabitation is as widely accepted by women as by men, a man knows that he has multiple options for finding a woman who will live with him. He doesn't have to commit to marriage to reap its benefits—companionship, sex, and reduced expenses. Ironically, had the woman refused to live with him, she might have retained her allure and been the person he asked to be his wife. However, with her agreeing merely to cohabit, the man remains uncommitted and available for a better prospect.

The woman also considers herself open to other men. That's why there's so much infidelity among cohabiting couples. In fact, both genders in a cohabiting relationship are much more likely than a married couple to be unfaithful.

The allure of cohabitation is grounded in a disturbing and ultimately crippling difference in the way men and women think about living together: Women cohabit to get a marriage proposal. Men cohabit for sex and money.

But living together sets up a relationship for failure. It's a trap. The only question, in most cases, is whether the relationship will fail before or after the wedding.

Studies show that half of cohabiting relationships end within fifteen months—without a wedding. That's largely why the number of never-married Americans jumped from 21 million in 1970 to 52 million in 2005. That's a 148 percent growth in the numbers of unwed Americans, triple the 46 percent growth of America's population in those decades.

On the other hand, one could argue, nearly half of cohabitations do result in marriage. But such couples face much greater odds of divorce—67 percent as opposed to the usual 45 percent for first marriages.

With more than an 80 percent chance of failure, both partners lose. Nor are these breakups painless, even if they occur before a marriage. Both genders, but particularly women, suffer from the effects of a "prenuptial divorce." Sex is bonding. Yet if a couple lives together without the long-term security of marriage, the physical intimacy that is intended to be a positive experience actually works against the relationship. A man and woman cannot cohabit without becoming "one," as Scripture puts it—joined together at a profound level—even if one or both partners have no plans for marriage.

When the relationship fails, either before the wedding or afterward, "couples do not simply separate; they tear," asserts Rev. Myles Munroe of Bahamas Faith Ministries in Nassau, holding up both hands with his fingers interlaced. He pulls them apart slowly, saying, "A part of you stays with the other person, and a part of them stays with you. That's why it is so painful."

As a consequence, women in particular feel used and embittered. What a woman hoped was a prelude to marriage ends badly and sadly.

She has squandered time she can never recapture. The inevitable result is that the freshness and idealism of her youth is lost to a man unwilling to make a full commitment.

Ironically, had she refused to move in with him, insisting on a traditional courtship, she might have successfully married the same man. Historically men have been more promiscuous than women. Women used to be a restraint on men's passions. If the woman had resisted the man's invitation to move in, he might well have decided to make a full commitment and marry her.

What women in this generation fail to understand is something their grandmothers knew instinctively: men marry women they respect. One way a woman can gain that respect is by refusing to have sex outside of marriage. Will some men not date her as a result? Of course. But arguably, they were not worth her time anyway.

If a woman compounds the moral compromise of sex before marriage by succumbing to a man's invitation to live together, he loses respect for her. It's a rule of human nature that's as real as the force of gravity: Respect must be earned. And respect in a relationship can be lost forever unless the woman has enough self-respect to decline an invitation to cohabit. Harriet and I know a woman, an adult child of divorce, who has lived with four men. She's now in her late thirties and has nothing to show for her failed relationships—no marriage and no children—and she's broken up with the fourth man as well.

Men know they can take their time finding a mate. They don't feel a sense of urgency because they don't have the same kind of time limit on their search for a partner that women do, whose biological clocks limit their childbearing years. Men can simply find younger partners. But in his self-absorption, a man may ruin a relationship with a woman that could have blossomed into a happy union had it begun with traditional courtship, living apart, followed by marriage.

Recently a woman confided, "We were together for three years.

We married only two months ago. Now he has moved out. What can I do?"

Cohabitation, which seems attractive at the outset, often leads to chaos and pain. It *is* evil. Millions of young women and men have pinned their hopes and dreams of marriage not on a ring and a wedding but on the quagmire of cohabitation. As a consequence, couples find their futures dashed upon the sharp rocks of "premarital divorce," or, later, real divorce.

CHAPTER 2

Why Couples Live Together

Do not set foot on the path of the wicked or walk in the way of evil men.

Proverbs 4:14

The United States is notable for having the world's highest divorce rate. . . . The risk of a marriage ending in divorce in the United States is close to 50 percent.

Dr. David Popenoe and Dr. Barbara Dafoe Whitehead,
The State of Our Unions, 2005

WHEN HARRIET AND I were married in 1965, it never occurred to us to live together before our wedding. In fact, when I tried to persuade her to move from New York City to Washington, near me, and live with her parents, she refused.

I shared a small townhouse in Georgetown then with two other single guys and worked as a *TIME* correspondent. She lived in New York with her sister and worked for TIME-LIFE Books. "Why not move back to D.C. and live with your folks?" I asked.

"Absolutely not," she responded. "I wouldn't think of moving unless we're married," she told me in no uncertain terms. "I don't want to move to Washington on the chance that you *might* marry me. It's too big a risk."

Boy, have things changed! Now 5.4 million couples are living together at any given time. In a year's time, between 7 million and 9 million couples have cohabited.

What's more, two-thirds of males aged eighteen to forty-four believe it's a good idea to cohabit before marrying, according to a study by the National Center for Health Statistics released in June 2006.

Why do so many couples cohabit? Let's explore both the rationalizations for living together and the deeper motivations that lead couples to do so.

COMMON RATIONALIZATIONS FOR COHABITING

Rationalization 1: We're in a Trial Marriage

The website www.cohabiting.org asks cohabiting individuals, "How would you describe your relationship?" Some 54 percent of 1,390 respondents, in an unscientific sample, said they were "testing" the relationship or were in a "trial marriage."[1] Yet when asked if they intended to marry their partner, only 61 percent said yes; 30 percent said maybe; and 4 percent said no.

The problem is, "You can't practice permanence," declares Dr. Barbara Markey, the primary creator of the FOCCUS Premarital Inventory. The only true commitment comes when a man and woman take the vows of marriage, marrying "for better, for worse, for richer, for poorer, in sickness and in health, to love and to cherish, till death us do part." It's easy to be married "for better . . . for richer . . . in health." True commitment comes during the times that are "for worse . . . for poorer . . . in sickness."

Given the widely publicized data that half of new marriages fail, it seems logical to have a "trial marriage" to "test the waters before tying the knot," according to Stacy and Wynne Whitman, coauthors of the book *Shacking Up.*

However, given the fact that less than half of cohabiting couples marry, and those who marry after living together are more likely to divorce than those who remained apart, this is more of a rationalization than carefully considered reasoning. A 1985 Columbia University study based on interviews of thirteen thousand participants and cited in *New Woman* magazine found that "only 26 percent of women surveyed and a scant 19 percent of the men married the person with whom they were living." Andrew Cherlin of Johns Hopkins University came to an even more discouraging conclusion: the proportion of cohabiting unions that end in marriage within three years dropped from 60 percent in the 1970s to about 33 percent in the 1990s."[2]

Rationalization 2: We Can't Afford to Live Apart

The number two reason couples live together, cited by 29 percent of those in the cohabiting.org survey, is convenience and economics. (Of course, the same savings could be achieved if each individual lived with a person of the same gender rather than moving in together as a couple.)

Hector and Teresa moved into a townhouse they purchased jointly six months before their wedding. He told me, "Since we are paying for our own wedding, we have to save money. One monthly mortgage payment is cheaper than two rents. Also, the lease expired on my apartment. So we decided to buy a condo, stop paying rent, and share a mortgage. A portion of our payments are paying off our mortgage, putting money into our own pocket, instead of the landlord's."

What Hector and Theresa had not considered is that buying a home together before marriage compounds the risks of living together. It's a major economic gamble. What if they break up before the wedding? How is the partner who moves out going to recoup his or her portion of the down payment and mortgage payments? If the couple had married and divorced, the property would likely be sold and any assets split fifty-fifty. The law protects the rights of divorced spouses; it does not protect separating cohabitors unless the couple has signed a legal agreement (Joint Tenants with Rights of Survivorship), which only one-tenth of cohabiting couples have done.[3] Cohabiting couples who jointly purchase property place themselves in an economic trap.

Cohabiting couples who share assets need to know that the divorce rate for those who marry after cohabiting is much higher than for those who never lived together. Yes, two *can* live together more cheaply than separately; but in the long run, living together outside of marriage can be far more costly emotionally, physically, and even financially. That's risky business.

Rationalization 3: I Don't Want to Be Lonely

The desire to be loved is "so overwhelming and strong that many will 'settle for' rather than choose someone." This is how cohabiting.org describes the excessive neediness to live with someone of the opposite gender exhibited by people in a "Linus Blanket" relationship. Such emotional neediness is the top reason for living together given by 13 percent of couples.[4] Typically, it's women who want this "blanket." Many feel so starved for security and intimacy that they'll accept almost anyone. And when conflicts arise, these women often give in rather than assert themselves. Fear of abandonment dominates the relationship. When the affair ends, as it usually does, the deserted partner feels used and abused—left in an extreme state of rejection, devaluation, and lowered self-esteem.

"Karen" did not love the man with whom she was living. Dr. Judith Wallerstein, author of *The Unexpected Legacy of Divorce,* interviewed her every five years since Karen's parents divorced twenty-five years earlier. Karen confessed, "You remember that when I was dating guys in college, I became very frightened that anyone I really liked would abandon me or be unfaithful, and that I would end up suffering like my mom and dad? Well, choosing Nick was safe because he has no education and no plans, which means that he'll always have fewer choices than me. I knew that if we lived together and maybe got married someday, I wouldn't ever have to worry about him walking out." With tears in her eyes, she added, "Nick is very kind and caring. I'm not used to that."[5]

Rationalization 4: Sex Is More Convenient

Perhaps surprisingly, the number of couples who live together purely for convenient sex is tiny—only 2 percent of the 1,390 couples participating in a survey on cohabiting.org.[6]

Rationalization 5: We Want Emancipation from Our Parents

About 1 percent of couples include a person who wants to leave a tumultuous home life and prove to parents that he or she can make independent choices and is no longer bound by parental constraints. But such a couple rarely has the discipline to work through their differences and resolve conflicts. It's not a relationship that's likely to lead to marriage.

UNDERLYING REASONS FOR COHABITATION

Conventional wisdom says it's a good idea to live with someone before getting married. Conventional wisdom is wrong.

"All a man's ways seem right to him," says Proverbs 21:2, "but the LORD weighs the heart." In contrast with the rationalizations for cohabiting, we've identified seven less-recognized underlying issues driving the twelvefold increase in the number of cohabiting couples—reasons even the couples themselves might not fully understand.

Underlying Reason 1: The Broken Home

Today's couples in their twenties and thirties distrust marriage. Since 1970, 42 million people have seen their parents divorce. These children are more likely to get divorced themselves. Since 1975 about 2.2 million marriages have been recorded each year—and 1.1 million divorces. For the third decade, half of marriages are ending in divorce. The Buster Generation, children of divorcing Baby Boomers, has lived the horrors of divorce and is wary of marriage for good reason.

From a young couple's point of view, marital success appears to be hit or miss—a crapshoot. So it's understandable that this generation lives together to test their relationships—to try to ensure compatibility. It seems like a reasonable thing to do. However, one consequence of so many couples living together is that the number of Americans who marry at all has fallen by 50 percent since 1970. And those who marry after living together are even more likely to divorce.

Teresa has a typical family history for many cohabitors:

> My mom is a single parent. She raised me by herself with the help of my grandmother. My father? I haven't seen him in many years. I never had a relationship with him. I wouldn't know him if I saw him on the street. By the time I was in college, he had not followed through on so many promises, it was easier for me not to deal with the heartache of disappointment. He'd say, "I'll buy you something for Christmas." But it never came.
>
> My mom remarried when I was six. It didn't work out. She divorced after a couple of years. Her husband was abusive. My mother said, "I'd rather be single." After that, she did not date, saying, "I don't have time for that."

Teresa had never witnessed a stable marriage. She never really knew her father. When her mother remarried, that marriage also failed. So Teresa had no template for a healthy marriage. Her images of intimacy and commitment had been distorted by her parents' dysfunctional example. She didn't have a true north on her emotional compass to guide her in forging a relationship with a man. Her anxiety led her to suggest to her boyfriend, Hector, that they live together before marrying, mistakenly perceiving that step as a safeguard against divorce.[7]

Sadly, this scenario is typical of millions of young adults. A million children a year witness a parental divorce. Like Teresa, many children experience two or more parental marital failures. Indeed, two-thirds of the children of divorce studied over twenty-five years experienced the agony of "multiple divorces and remarriages of one or both of their parents," according to the authors of *The Unexpected Legacy of Divorce*. Millions also have had to endure a series of their parents' live-in lovers, compounding the fear that relationships are doomed. The children declare flatly, "The day my parents divorced is the day my childhood ended."[8]

Being raised in a fatherless home is a common element in the family history of many cohabiting couples. That experience breeds a fear of failure in marriage as adults, which influences their capacity to build a lasting marriage. As Dr. Wade Horn, child psychologist and former assistant secretary of the U.S. Department of Health and Human Services, has said, "Ours is a divorce-phobic generation."

Understandably, then, these grown children often live with a prospective mate to try to assess whether they think the relationship is marriage-worthy. And cohabitation is not going away, according to University of Michigan sociologist Pamela Smock, Ph.D. and her colleague Wendy Manning, Ph.D.: "Cohabitation has become a normative part of the life course of young Americans. The percentage of marriages preceded by cohabitation rose from about 10% for those marrying between 1965 and 1974 to well over 50% for those marrying between 1990 and 1994."[9] "The percentage of women in their late 30s who report having cohabited at least once rose from 30% in 1987 to 48% in 1995."[10]

Smock and Manning added that today's young people "think it would idiotic not to live with someone before marriage. They don't want to end up the way their parents or older relatives did, which is divorced."

By contrast, children growing up in a two-parent home rarely experience such doubts and fears. They assume they will find a mate for life and that they can select one through a dating process. Such a person is far less likely to cohabit than one who grew up in the home of a divorced or a never-married parent.

Of course, many adult children of divorce do create solid marriages. The April 15, 2007, *New York Times* reported the marriage of David Milowitz to Laura Shoop. Milowitz confessed to the reporter, "I didn't really want a relationship and I never really thought I was going to get married. My parents being divorced made me lose total faith in the whole concept of marriage." Then he met Shoop, a fellow dancer who was too beautiful not to pursue. However, his fear of relationship failure led him to suggest that they see a therapist. Shoop's parents had been married thirty-seven years, so she wasn't plagued by the same fears; but she cooperated, to a happy ending.

Underlying Reason 2: Lack of Male Commitment

A second major reason millions of unmarried American couples cohabit is that many men won't commit to marriage without first living with a woman. Drs. Barbara Dafoe Whitehead and David Popenoe, of the National Marriage Project at Rutgers University, blame the men. Based on focus-group discussions with young, heterosexual, unmarried men in New Jersey, Chicago, Washington, D.C., and Houston, they conclude in an essay, "Why Men Won't Commit" (part of their report *The State of Our Unions, 2002*): "Men experience few social pressures to marry, gain many of the benefits of marriage by cohabiting with a romantic partner, and are ever more reluctant to commit to marriage in their early adult years." They found that 44 percent of single men aged twenty to twenty-nine say they would not marry a woman unless she agreed to cohabit first. Furthermore, while men express a desire to marry at some point, they're in no hurry.[11]

This major gender difference is not generally recognized. The following letter posted at cohabiting.org accurately depicts the tension between women and men in cohabiting relationships:

> I am in a cohabiting relationship going on a year now and I love the person dearly but living together is just not enough for me anymore and I want marriage but in a way I think that he is just comfortable the way things are now and I feel as if he could make me wait forever. I will never do this again should my boyfriend and I break up. I just feel like I am doing all that a wife does and more and I don't get anything out of it. The stats scare me considering that we are currently engaged I just am frightened. I don't even want to marry him now. I just want to move out and start over.[12]

Fear may be a factor underlying the stated reasons for the unwillingness of many men to commit. The essay authors report, "For the young men in these groups, the early adult years are a time of insecure job and residential attachment." For example, more than half had changed jobs in the past five years, and 20 percent had been fired. Their living arrangements also are fluid and unstable. They may live with other single men, then try cohabiting, then move back into their parents' home.[13]

Besides stability issues, fear can arise over other things. If a woman

Ten Reasons Why Men Won't Commit

The National Marriage Project lists these top ten reasons why men won't commit:[14]

1. "They can get sex without marriage more easily than in times past." As my mother used to tell my sister in the 1950s, "If you give him free milk, why would he buy the cow?"

2. "They can enjoy the benefits of having a wife by cohabiting rather than marrying." Men like the convenience of an easily available sex partner and the economies of shared living. They believe living together is a way to avoid an unhappy marriage and eventual divorce. Men believe this is the only way to test compatibility for marriage.

3. "They want to avoid divorce and its financial risks." They feel their assets are better protected if they cohabit rather than marry, that an ex-wife will "take you for all you've got."

4. "They want to wait until they are older to have children." Easy for them to do. "Unlike women, they have no biological clock to impose a strict time limit on fertility," says the National Marriage Project. Men are indifferent to women's time pressures. As one young man observed, "That's their issue."

5. "They fear that marriage will require too many changes and compromises." Men have become accustomed to

(continued)

21

their own space and routines and resent women who try to change them. They're looking for a woman so compatible that they won't have to change for her.

6. "They are waiting for the perfect soul mate and she hasn't yet appeared." Men don't want to settle for second best in their choice of a marriage partner. However, they don't have the same standards for a live-in girlfriend. Indeed, "They see her as a second-best partner while they continue to look for a soul mate." There is nothing wrong with looking for a soul mate, but cohabiting with someone first is no way to find #1.

7. "They face few social pressures to marry." Traditional pressures from the church, employers, society, and parents have evaporated.

8. "They are reluctant to marry a woman who already has children."

9. "They want to own a house before they get a wife." Curiously, few of the men interviewed for this study are homeowners.

10. "They want to enjoy single life as long as they can." They are having lots of fun with no responsibilities. Yet 325,000 cohabiting men father children a year. Without the wedding ring, the unmarried father is likely to abandon the mother of his children to search for his soul mate.

talks about looking forward to having children, some men fear that she will "trick" them into fathering a child for whom they will be responsible. Others worry that a woman who gets pregnant after casual sex might deny them the opportunity to get to know and bond with a child they are legally required to support. Men also are turned off if a woman asks questions about money. They fear "gold diggers"—women they suspect are evaluating them on the basis of their current income, their possessions, or their earning potential.

If men can overcome these fears, many will suggest living together as a good way to get to know each other better, since they (incorrectly) believe "it's the little things" that can wreck a marriage. In the twenty-first century, cohabitation has become the next step after dating. "Why Men Won't Commit" reports that close to a third of the sixty men between ages twenty and twenty-nine participating in focus groups had already lived with a woman outside of marriage.[15] For millions of men it's a conscious postponement of serious consideration of marriage. No wonder the number of never-married Americans jumped from 21 million in 1970 to 52 million in 2005—a 148 percent increase. And the rise in number of never-marrieds can't simply be attributed to having a higher number of Americans overall: the increase is more than triple the rate of population growth (46 percent) during that same time period.

Ironically, "Men were less dedicated in their marriages if they had lived with their partners before marriage," according to Dr. Scott Stanley in his 2005 book, *The Power of Commitment*.[16] So the very insistence by men that women live with them before marriage undermines their own capacity for marital commitment.

Underlying Reason 3: Cultural Pressure

Until recently American society frowned upon couples living together outside of wedlock. The culture reflected Judeo-Christian values in a nation where two-thirds of Americans are members of a church, according to a Gallup Poll. "Today the pendulum has swung to the other extreme," writes David Gudgel in *Before You Live Together*. He continues:

If two people choose *not* to live together before marriage, many think they are strange—out of step, old-fashioned, a quart low.

The societal, parental and religious influences and pressures that once held a strong hand in keeping couples apart until marriage have weakened. When the television show *Three's Company* appeared in 1977, most Americans were shocked. In the show, two single women and a single man share an apartment. Even though the three characters were not physically involved, it was rare that individuals of the opposite sex would live together under the same roof. Today that concern is laughable. . . .

Today there is even social pressure *to* live together. Couples hear two myths, "Everyone else is doing it. How else will you know if you should get married?"[17]

In the 2003–2004 television season, networks featured so-called reality shows not on marriage but on weddings and the hunt for a sexy, rich mate, such as *Joe Millionaire.* Other shows included *The Bachelor, Who Wants to Marry a Millionaire?, For Love or Money,* and *Who Wants to Marry My Dad?* Shows featured contests in which people decided whom they should marry based on appearance and money. Character, morals, and personal achievement were ignored. While most adults regard these shows as silly fantasies, they *are* viewed by some young people as representative of how choices are made about whom to marry and of what they should look for in a future mate.

Celebrities, often regarded as cultural role models (such as Oprah, who cohabits with Stedman), give social sanction to what used to be called "living in sin" or "shacking up." Now the neutral term "living together" has replaced pejorative phrases that clearly communicated disapproval of unwed partners living as married couples. Goldie Hawn, who celebrated her sixtieth birthday with "longtime love Kurt Russell," as *AARP Magazine* put it, has cohabited for more than twenty years. The couple has a nineteen-year-old son and are "one of Hollywood's most enduring movie star couples." The culture has become a harmful force, blindly endorsing cohabitation as if it posed little or no risk.

Curiously, the one element of society expected to oppose living together—organized religion—has been oddly mute. Many clergy simply ignore the issue. Other than the National Marriage Project at Rutgers, which publishes *The State of Our Unions* annually, most of the academic community has been similarly silent (other than some scholars quoted here), as have politicians.

Underlying Reason 4: Drift

To many couples, moving in with someone of the opposite sex is not a great rubicon that is crossed. Most drift into cohabitation. He spends weekends at her apartment. She suggests, "Why not move the rest of your stuff over here? Then we can see each other every night and also save money."

In this scenario, the issue of marriage is sidestepped. It simply is not discussed. She presumes that his moving in means that he's making a greater commitment that could lead to marriage. Chances are, he has no intention of proposing.

In his insightful 2005 book *Living Together: A Guide to Counseling Unmarried Couples,* Jeff Van Goethem asks:

> Is it really wise for cohabitors not to discuss with one another such issues as responsibilities, obligations, future goals, and marriage? Books are being published today urging cohabiting couples to enter into written contracts that spell out property rights, bill-paying responsibilities, rules for debt-encumbrance, inheritance issues, and other

practical concerns. Doesn't a failure to agree on the nature of the relationship increase the risk of misunderstanding, disappointment, and heartbreak? Marriage tends to eliminate many such concerns, since both parties understand exactly what they're committing themselves to.[18]

If more couples openly and clearly discussed their expectations and plans before deciding to live together, fewer couples would be deceived into thinking their partner felt the same way they did, leading to fewer couples cohabiting and, perhaps, more of those who do having relationships that lasted.

Consider Jan and Jack, who met each other on a Christian website in January 2005 and started dating that month. They lived about sixty miles from each other, at opposite ends of the Washington metropolitan area. Jack, twenty-four, a truck driver, lived in a rented house with male friends. Jan, twenty-seven, lived with her parents until they retired and moved west. Then she moved into an apartment paid for by her father. She was studying to become a personal chef and working part-time as a waitress. For Jack, it was a long drive around the congested Washington Beltway to visit Jan. In February he began spending weekends with her; by March he had moved into her apartment.

Neither could see a reason not to move in together, even though deep personal commitment was absent. They weren't engaged. "I'm not sure why we started," Jack told Harriet and me as we began mentoring them in the summer of 2005. "It was for many reasons. One was that I love you," he told Jan. "I want to be with you. Second was a financial thing." Jan added, "I was a female living alone. I don't have a lot of confidence in my ability to make decisions." Not powerful reasons to live together.

Drift was part of the reason this couple began cohabiting. Most couples slide into cohabiting without a marriage commitment, and these are the ones most likely to either break up before a wedding or to divorce later.

As recently as the 1960s, nearly half of women were virgins when they married. The conviction that premarital sex was wrong was widespread. But with the availability of birth control pills, premarital sex became more common. When that barrier fell, dating quickly led to intercourse. Casual sex became the norm.

Two unhealthy aberrations ensued. First came the phenomenon, especially on college campuses, of "hooking up"—a man meets a woman, they have a few drinks, and then have sex, with virtually no relationship at all. Thus, the sexual act, which Scripture says should be reserved for marriage, is further cheapened. Often couples don't even date after hooking up.

The second unhealthy consequence of casual sex is that it often leads to cohabitation. But drifting in is much easier than pulling out.

Couples commonly have the misperception that it will be just as easy to end a cohabitation arrangement as it was to begin one. However, Stanley argues in *The Power of Commitment* that living together increases constraints, making it harder to end a relationship than if a couple is merely dating but living separately. A boyfriend brings over some clothes and toiletries, and soon a whole dresser. Couples start making investments together—a bed, a couch, a pet. Inertia sets in, keeping some couples together longer than is healthy simply because it's hard to leave when they share a home and other possessions. "These couples are sliding, not deciding, their way into marriage," Stanley observes. "The inertia theory suggests that couples who are at the greatest risk are those who are in love but aren't sure they want a future together. People don't realize that it's much harder to break off the relationship once they move in together. Further, many couples have children (planned or not) when they live together, and that makes it even more gut-wrenching to contemplate ending the relationship,"[19] Stanley asserts.

"Once their lives are thoroughly entangled, some couples may decide to wed more out of guilt or fear than love," writes Nancy Wartik in "The Perils of Playing House," an article in the July/August 2005 issue of *Psychology Today*. She quotes New York psychiatrist John Jacobs: "I know a lot of men who've been living with women for a couple of years, and they're very ambivalent about marrying them. What sways them is a feeling they owe it to her. She'll be back on the market and she's older. He's taken up a lot of her time."[20]

Those are not good reasons to marry.

Psychology Today's blunt conclusion: "Cohabitation may lead you to wed for all the wrong reasons—or turn into a one-way trip to splitsville."

Underlying Reason 5: Unwise Parenting

Surprisingly, a growing number of parents see nothing wrong with their adult children cohabiting. In the case of Jan and Jack, neither set of parents objected to their living together. In fact, Jan's father welcomed the idea of having someone share his daughter's rent, since it meant he could pay less.

During a marriage preparation class we led at our church in Bethesda, Maryland, Harriet told me, "The couple in the front row is living together." In my opening remarks I said that our church would not knowingly marry couples who were cohabiting. "However," I added, "cohabiting couples are welcome to attend our premarital program and be assigned a Mentor Couple, who will give you a marriage inventory, help you better understand your relationship, and teach you problem-solving skills."

Later, the young man confessed that they were cohabiting. "But I want you to know it was not my idea but that of my future father-in-law. He wanted us to try out the relationship, so he invited me to move into her bedroom in their home. He told me he was spending $35,000 on the wedding, and he insisted on making sure our marriage would last."

I was thunderstruck. Evidently the culture had changed so much that some parents were actually encouraging cohabitation under their own roofs! Nevertheless, I invited the young couple to meet for a private conversation about the risks they were running. They agreed to come, but two days later Jim called to say that his fiancée's parents planned to join them.

We asked our pastor if he would be willing to host the meeting in his office. He had set the standard that he would not knowingly marry anyone who was living together, so it was appropriate to have him involved in this confrontation. And that's exactly what it was.

When Harriet and I arrived at the church, we heard shouting. The parents had arrived early and were screaming. Upon walking into the pastor's office, we were accosted by "Mrs. Jones": "Look at my daughter's eyes. She has been crying for days. She was so happy to be engaged, and loved their Mentor Couple. Then you inserted yourself into this situation. Mr. McManus, you have ruined her wedding. What right have you got to come under our roof and tell our family how they are supposed to live and behave? This is a matter between my daughter, her fiancé, us, and God."

The pastor remained calm and turned to the young couple. "Of course, I'm going to marry you. And of course, Jim, you're going to move out of her bedroom. I will meet with you privately next week to discuss the details."

Then he turned to the Joneses, who had not attended church in seven years, and said, "I believe you will see that God has something in this for you, too."

Jim did move out. The young couple met with their Mentor Couple not the expected five times but ten times. Their scores on the premarital inventory were dismal—even regarding sex. But as they talked through their issues, the quality of their relationship improved so dramatically that the grateful couple invited their Mentor Couple to participate in their wedding. They also later invited the mentors to the christening of their first child. Even the Joneses were impressed with how their daughter was prepared for marriage—so much so that they became active members of the church.

The mentoring process positively impacted three generations: the young couple, their children (who now attend Sunday school), and the young woman's parents.

Underlying Reason 6: Denial

Denial is strong in couples living together or considering cohabitation. When we first met with Hector and Teresa as their mentors, we encouraged them to consider moving apart. "Whether one looks at this from a biblical or a secular perspective, the overwhelming evidence suggests that living together is unwise." I provided data to back up my assertion.

Hector listened politely and then stoutly disputed that any of what I said applied to them: "We're not going to be one of those statistics."

Clearly, they were in denial about the risks of cohabitation, even when evidence was presented by knowledgeable and caring mentors. Data was brushed aside like an irritating fly.

Ironically, Hector and Teresa had a heated argument that very evening and came precariously close to breaking their engagement.

Underlying Reason 7: Government-Subsidized Cohabitation

A growing group of cohabiting couples are retired individuals who live together to avoid losing Social Security benefits. "We want to marry," a seventy-four-year-old man told me. "But my partner would lose her Social Security survivor's benefits."

Dorian Solot, on CBS's *The Early Show*, said: "The number of unmarried senior couples has increased 60 percent in the last decade. They're imitating their grandchildren."[21] Solot is a former director of the Alternatives to Marriage Project. Fortunately, the actual number of cohabiting seniors is still relatively small: 280,000 couples over age 65 in 2006, according to Census. Most elders do marry, not cohabit. This may cost a loss of income, but it is the right thing to do. Cohabiting would set a bad example for their children and grandchildren.

More important, the *government actually subsidizes cohabitation of low-income couples.* The Institute for American Values documented a case of a California father who earned $14,556, out of which he paid $1,884 in taxes plus $2,400 for child support. His lover, a mother of two, worked part-time, earning $7,284. However, if the couple remains unmarried, she receives $5,280 a year in welfare, $7,944 in housing subsidies, and $1,368 in food stamps. She pays no income tax, yet receives a $2,352 Earned Income Tax Credit (EITC) check from the IRS. That adds up to $16,944 in government subsidies for a single mom with two kids. Even after deducting for the man's taxes and child support, the couple has an annual income of $34,500. If they marry, he would no longer pay child support, but the woman would lose much of her welfare, housing subsidy, food stamps, and EITC, which would reduce the couple's income to $30,624.[22]

Thus, the government is essentially paying this couple nearly $4,000 a year *not* to marry.

The government's assumption is that the woman doesn't need as much subsidy if she has access to the man's income, which she presumably would if they were married. However, if they cohabit rather than marry, she likely has access to his income plus the $4,000.

This is perverse public policy that ought to be reversed.

In reality, since cohabitation lasts only fifteen months on average, the longer-term economic attractiveness of living together really is not the glue it appears to be before moving in together.

To its credit, the George W. Bush Administration eliminated a provision in the tax code that made cohabitation attractive to middle-income earners. If, for example, a teacher earning $30,000 married a teacher who also earns $30,000, their combined income tax used to increase if they married. Also, their tax deductions for charitable contributions were worth less if they married. The Bush tax cut passed by Congress in 2001 eliminated those marriage penalties for middle-income couples. However, the measure was slowly phased in during this decade and is scheduled to sunset in 2010 unless Congress passes new enabling legislation. With a Democratic Congress as of 2007–2008, the outcome is unclear.

In any case, subsidies to the poor who cohabit are much larger, proportionally, than the marriage penalty once paid by middle-income spouses. The federal government needs to address the disincentive to marry that is built into the EITC, Social Security, food stamps, Medicaid, and other programs. Government should create economic conditions that encourage marriage, not cohabitation. It should promote morality, not immorality.

As Senator Sam Brownback (R-Kans.) put it, "We should support marriage, not tax it. It is wrong to tax welfare benefits just because someone gets married. Marriage remains the best place to raise children—not the only place, but the best place."[23]

CHAPTER 3
Risks of Cohabitation

Can a man scoop fire into his lap without his clothes being burned? Can a man walk on hot coals without his feet being scorched?

Proverbs 6:27–28

The truth is that wherever a man lies with a woman, whether they like it or not, a transcendental relation is set up between them which must be eternally enjoyed or eternally endured.

C. S. Lewis, *The Screwtape Letters*

IN 2004, TWO producers for ABC's *Good Morning America* asked if they could follow our mentoring of a premarital couple for their audience. "Belinda," an attorney in her mid-thirties, wanted us to mentor her and her boyfriend. She planned to marry "Peter," who processed car loans. The couple had been dating for only five months and had "met" on the Internet. But she spoke with joy and confidence about the relationship. She was quite willing to allow *Good Morning America* to videotape the mentoring experience and thought Peter would agree. However, in our first conversation she said she was having difficulty contacting him.

I was puzzled. I had never heard of an engaged couple having trouble reaching each other.

Belinda said that Peter had been married before and had a six-year-old son. His former wife, a physician, had been in an auto accident in January, and he had gone back to New Jersey to arrange for her care. Yet it was odd that he had been out of touch with Belinda for several days.

I asked, "Are you living together?"

"Yes, but we've only just begun," she answered.

"That is very unwise," I replied, and explained: "Couples who live together increase their odds of divorce."

"Really? Well, we just drifted into this. It's not something we consciously decided to do. I think I'll end it."

Three days later, I finally spoke with Peter and set up the videotape session for a week later. However, at 1:15 p.m. the day of the scheduled session, a distraught Belinda called to say, "I'm sorry, but we're going to have to cancel our session tonight. I expected Peter to be here this morning, but he never showed up, and I can't reach him on his cell phone."

"Did you call him at work?" I asked.

"Well, he only started with this auto dealership yesterday. When I called there, no one had heard of him."

The situation was sounding odder by the minute. "I don't think it's wise to proceed, even if he were to show up now," I said. "Something is fundamentally wrong here. We're going to have to get another couple." She understood.

Out of concern for her, I called Belinda the next day. She still had not heard from Peter and was shaken by the experience. She said she had him move out of the apartment two days earlier. "I didn't think it was right for us to live together," she said. "However, I'm worried because some of my possessions are gone." That was alarming.

Two days after the original planned visit, Belinda called with shocking news. "I've learned that Peter has been married *three* times and has *six* children he's supposed to be supporting. A seventh is on the way. There are *warrants for his arrest in three states for non–child support*. He has also been convicted in Virginia of embezzling and was on probation. He obviously didn't want to be seen on *Good Morning America*. He might have been arrested.

"Also, I'm missing a pair of diamond earrings, a diamond pin, leather coat, and other things. I've called the police and reported these items stolen. Peter said he was an ordained minister, but apparently he just uses that to build trust."

"How did you discover his sordid past?" I asked.

"A girlfriend suggested that I check my phone bills to see if he made any calls on my phone when he was here. I found numbers of women who were only too willing to tell me what he had done to them."

Here was a modern Don Juan who knew how to manipulate the Internet to lure affluent women in their thirties, gain their confidence, seduce them, move in, steal from them—and move on to repeat the cycle again on another lonely, unsuspecting victim. Who knows how many women he'd met on the Internet and duped? He had married three times and was prepared to do so again.

Belinda was saved by her call to us and by *Good Morning America*. Countless other women are not so fortunate. They meet someone on the Internet, slip into cohabitation thinking it will lead to marriage, and end up being sadder—but not necessarily wiser.

SPECIAL RISKS FOR WOMEN

While cohabitation is very popular, it's an extremely risky lifestyle. Although the consequences of living together outside of marriage affect both partners, some disproportionately impact women and children. Judith Krantz, writing in *Cosmopolitan* in 1976, explained why women who cohabit are at high risk:

When a woman lives with a man without the couple's making mutual and wholehearted investment of themselves implicitly in what is now so scornfully called a "little piece of paper"—i.e., a marriage certificate—she immediately loses the following things: her independence, her freedom to make choices, her privacy, all of her mystery, any practical bargaining position in the power struggle of love . . . the prospect of having a child other than an illegitimate one, and the protection of the law.[1]

According to cohabiting.org, compared to married women, cohabiting women

- are three times as likely to suffer depression, according to the National Institute for Mental Health;
- suffer from neurotic disorders (25 percent) more than married women (15 percent);
- are "more irritable, anxious, worried and unhappy" than married women.[2]

The reason cohabiting women are unhappy is that the men hold a power of sorts over them. A woman keeps hoping her partner will ask her to marry him. The longer he fails to do so, the unhappier she becomes.

Let's take a look at some more special risks for cohabiting women.

THE BURDEN OF CONDITIONAL LOVE AND A PERFORMANCE-BASED RELATIONSHIP

Consider a typical cohabiting situation. Two people love each other and decide to move in together to test the relationship. They think love might lead to marriage, but they want a greater sense of certainty. Essentially, it's a tryout—an audition of sorts. However, how will each person know if his or her partner will make a lifelong marriage mate? They're trying to find out how compatible they are, and it all depends on whether the partner is meeting their expectations.

That expectation, according to David Gudgel in *Before You Live Together,* forces the couple into a "performance-based relationship. Each person attempts to earn the other's love through achievement. Each evaluates whether the other lives up to his or her expectations."[3]

Gudgel explains:

Two words characterize performance-based relationships: "if" and "then." Whether you want to admit it, when two people live together before marriage they are thinking:

- *If* you make me feel loved, *then* I'll marry you.
- *If* you satisfy me sexually, *then* I'll marry you.
- *If* you treat me with respect, *then* I'll marry you.
- *If* you make me happy, *then* I'll marry you.
- *If* you make something of yourself, *then* I'll marry you.
- *If* you fulfill my needs, *then* I'll marry you.
- *If* you like what I like, *then* I'll marry you.
- *If* you don't do things that get on my nerves, *then* I'll marry you.[4]

It's reasonable to make a decision about whether to marry someone based on whether he or she makes you feel loved or happy. However, Gudgel argues that this approach to a fulfilling love is flawed.

In cohabitation, individuals usually focus on *obtaining satisfaction from the other person.* However, in marriage, spouses tend to focus more on *giving satisfaction to the other person.* In the process of giving to one's spouse, the giver receives joy as a by-product.

Love in a marriage is an *investment.* In cohabitation it's a *gamble.*

Cohabitation is *conditional.* Marriage is based on *permanence.*

These are radically different psychological premises for a relationship.

True love is selfless. Cohabitation is based on *selfishness:* how will this relationship satisfy *me?* True love seeks to serve the other person, not to use him or her. Pressing for sex before marriage—while it is widely accepted in today's culture—is selfish, not selfless.

In *Campus Life* (February 1996), Jim Long wrote: "Love can fool you. Your feelings can trick you. The line between love and infatuation is thin. And frankly, sex confuses everything. To be physically involved clouds the issue. It makes you feel closer than you really are. It makes you feel as if you are actually in love. Maybe so. Maybe not."

Ask a couple in a long-term, fulfilling marriage, "How would you define love?" and they will speak of unconditional love—their deep, abiding commitment to one another and their willingness to sacrifice to help each other fulfill their needs and goals.

True love in Scripture is not described as a feeling but as a decision. In 1 Corinthians 13:4–7, the most eloquent description of love in the New Testament, we find fifteen characteristics of godly, unconditional love—all of which require an act of the will: "Love is patient, love is kind. It does not envy, it does not boast, it is not proud. It is not rude, it is not self-seeking, it is not easily angered, it keeps no record of wrongs. Love does not delight in evil but rejoices with the truth. It always protects, always trusts, always hopes, always perseveres."

UNREALISTIC EXPECTATIONS

Men and women choose to cohabit for very different reasons. Rarely do couples discuss their underlying motivations for cohabiting. The only things both partners have likely agreed upon is that living together would save on rent. Often the woman views cohabitation as a stepping-stone to marriage. She presumes her boyfriend feels the same way. But men usually choose to live with women essentially for convenience—available sex and shared expenses. Such differing expectations inevitably lead to conflict.

Some men demand sex as evidence of love, which is patently exploitative. He's looking out for himself, at her expense. How she feels is often of little concern to him. He presumes their living together entitles him to sex on demand. One study revealed that 40 percent of cohabiting women were forced into sex.[5] Even if the couple marries, such a man may become a dominating, abusive tyrant.

BEING USED . . .

Cohabitors without plans to marry are more inclined to have an unfair division of labor than married couples, according to a study by Penn State professor Dr. Alan Booth and doctoral student Susan L. Brown.[6]

When they first move in together, most couples intend to split expenses fifty-fifty. However, women often pay more than their share of the expenses, so they are actually supporting the men. Furthermore, what may begin as an egalitarian relationship in which both genders supposedly share household tasks equally typically ends up as a situation in which women do most of the cleaning, cooking, and laundry. Such a relationship is very convenient—for men.

"Melody," thirty-nine, a graduate of New York's Fashion Institute of Technology, is an accomplished artist. She lived with "Paul," who didn't have a job. "He liked to gamble, drink, and do drugs," said Melody. "What attracted me to him was all physical. He is six feet tall, a good dresser, charming, nice—but not nice to women. I thought I could change him to be a person who was responsible, caring, and loving. He was good to me at first, but he only wanted to sit home, play video games, have friends over. I cooked and paid the bills."

She lived with Paul for six years. "He did not pay any rent," she recalled. "I thought I was in love. I felt I could change him." Now those years (and the money and energy she spent) are gone, and Melody has nothing to show for her investment in Paul.

Still need to be convinced?

Jen wrote to cohabiting.org:

> I lived with my bf [boyfriend] for one year and then moved back home. He followed and stays at my place 6 nights a week. [He doesn't] share any finances, food or otherwise. He wants to get married when my child leaves home someday (she's 17) or we can get married now and keep separate places and finances. He fixes some minor repairs at my house, but not if they are going to cost him. I am [a] single parent and can't afford enough groceries, much less repairs. Right now my front door is broken and won't lock, and he won't repair it till I can afford a new door. He thinks he is right about this? I am about to end it but feel like he will think it's because of money. Help!!![7]

Why didn't she throw him out long ago? She pays the rent and buys all the groceries on some vague promise that he might marry her when her daughter leaves. He can't even repair the door. Perhaps she's so lonely, she'll accept anything. But what lesson is this teaching Jen's daughter about relationships? One in ten cohabiting couples is in a "Linus Blanket" relationship such as this.

… AND ABUSED (THE HIGH RISK OF VIOLENCE AMONG COHABITORS)

Melody knew firsthand how cohabitation can leave one used *and* abused. She told us, "The first man I lived with, I knew it would not work out. When I wanted out of the relationship, he would stop me." She fled, but "he could not deal with it. He stalked me, and slapped me in front of my friends. I lived with him almost a year. Half the time I moved out of my own apartment and stayed with my mother."

Her second live-in relationship wasn't much better: "He abused me too. He had a violent streak when he was drunk."

At least Melody claims to have learned her lesson, even if it was the hard way. She says she will never live with another man unless she marries him.

Women who agree to cohabit unwittingly make themselves vulnerable candidates for domestic violence. Two decades ago (September 5, 1988) *TIME* magazine reported that "In almost two dozen recent studies, experts across the country estimate that an average of 30 percent of all unmarried individuals, whether dating or living together, have been involved in physical aggression with the opposite sex. *Couples who live together may be the most violent of all.*"

Numerous recent studies document that physical attacks among cohabiting couples are much more common than among married couples. Dr. Jan Stets of Washington State University, a noted researcher on cohabitation, found evidence that "aggression is at least twice as common among cohabitors as it is among married partners."[8] Actually, her research indicates the risk almost triples: "Approximately 14 percent of those who cohabit admit to hitting, shoving or throwing things at their partner during the past year compared to 5 percent of married people."[9] Linda Waite, professor of Sociology at the University of Chicago, reports almost identical ratios: 13 percent of cohabitors said that arguments became physical, with "hitting, shoving, and throwing things," over the last year, versus 4 percent of those married.[10]

The Family Violence Research Program at the University of New Hampshire reported that among 2,143 adults, "Cohabitors are much more violent than marrieds." The overall rates for "severe" violence was nearly *five times higher for cohabitors* compared with those for married couples. The researchers' conclusion? Marriage inhibits male violence.[11] Statscan, a Canadian government statistical agency, reported that "in a one-year period, one in every five women who live in common law is assaulted, and those with male partners under 25 are at most risk."

More important, murder is much more frequent among unwed couples. The National Crime Victimization Survey of the U.S. Justice Department reports that of all violent crimes against women committed by relatives or intimate partners between 1979 and 1987, about 65 percent were committed by either a boyfriend or an ex-husband. Only 9 percent were committed by husbands.

The *Washington Post* featured a series of stories in December 2004 about 1,367 "maternal homicides," in which a pregnant woman or one who had just given birth was murdered. Two-thirds of those cases involved unmarried women. Only 36 percent of the women murdered were married.

And the danger doesn't end when the relationship does. Women are eighteen times more likely to be assaulted by their male cohabitor after breaking up than they would be by a spouse.

Edgar Carrasquillo, forty-five, had been the live-in lover of Debra Smaniotto, forty-three, for two years in Vineland, New Jersey. Neighbors called him "very friendly." One said, "If you needed help with your groceries, he'd carry them. If it snowed, he shoveled the sidewalk." The couple broke up but remained so friendly that he helped her buy groceries on March 3, 2007, and departed. About forty-five minutes later, Smaniotto's new live-in lover, Bruce Bertoldi, forty-seven, arrived. Hours later, Smaniotto and Bertoldi lay dead in her condominium, and Carrasquillo killed himself near her mailbox.

The evidence is persuasive that women who cohabit are at much

Violence Between Intimate Partners

The Bureau of Justice Statistics issued a special report, "Intimate Partner Violence and Age of Victim, 1993–99," with these facts:

- Intimate male partners murdered 1,218 women in 1999 (while only 424 women murdered men).
- That same year, 671,110 female partners were victims of violent crime (compared with only 120,100 males).
- Married women face the smallest risk: of those aged twenty to twenty-four, only 8 per 1,000 were victimized.
- Among those never married, 20 per 1,000 women were victimized—*that's 2.5 times the rate of married women.*
- Women who break up with a cohabiting partner are at greatest risk—*eighteen times that of married women.* Of unmarried women aged twenty to twenty-four who separated from a partner, 151 per 1,000 were victimized. For those aged twenty-five to thirty-four, the ratio was 118 per 1,000.[12]

higher risk of being physically abused than women who move in with men only after marriage.

SPECIAL RISKS FOR CHILDREN

Census reports show that half of previously married cohabitors and 35 percent of never-married couples living together have children in the household. In fact, a surprising 41 percent of all cohabiting couples in 2003 had children under the age of eighteen living with them. That's virtually *equal* to the 46 percent of married couples who had children living with them.[13]

In 1970, 196,000 cohabiting couples had children living with them. By 2005 that number had increased tenfold—*1,000 percent*—to 1,954,000.[14]

Number of Unmarried Couple Households with Children[15]

Year	Number
1970	196,000
1980	431,000
1990	891,000
1995	1,319,000
1998	1,520,000
2005	1,954,000

A striking 86 percent of unmarried parents are cohabiting or are romantically involved, according to a study done for the Heritage Foundation.[16] "In other words, 86 percent of the out-of-wedlock births are to couples—unmarried couples, but couples nonetheless,"[17] according to research conducted by Columbia University's Social Indicators Survey Center and Princeton University's Center for Research on Child Wellbeing.

Fragile Families Research Associates, which interviewed 3,712 parents of children born to unmarried parents in cities with populations of 200,000 or more, found that at the time of the birth of their child, 70 percent of the mothers and 77 percent of the fathers believed their odds of marrying were high. Yet twelve to eighteen months later, only 12 percent of couples had married.

The public tends to blame rising out-of-wedlock birth rates on irresponsible single women. However, the aforementioned research indicates that cohabitation is the driving force behind many unwed births. And those birth rates are soaring. As indicated in the following table, the number of babies born out of wedlock has increased nearly sevenfold, from 224,000 in 1960 to 1,525,345 in 2005. This 1.5-million figure is the highest number of out-of-wedlock births ever recorded and accounts for 37.4 percent of all births.[18] Fully 55 percent of all births for women aged twenty to twenty-four were out of wedlock, 28 percent for those aged twenty-five to twenty-nine.

Births to Unwed Mothers[19]

Year	Out-of-Wedlock Births
1960	224,000
1970	398,000
1980	666,000
1990	1,165,000
2000	1,347,000
2005	1,525,345

What does a soaring out-of-wedlock birth rate mean for child well-being?

Risk of Delinquency

Children born out of wedlock are at much greater risk of failure than other children—greater risk even than children of divorce. For example, the Heritage Foundation reports that whereas a child of divorce is twelve times more likely to be jailed than one from an intact family home, a child of a nonmarriage is *twenty-two times more likely to be incarcerated.*[20]

Economic Disadvantage

Children of cohabiting parents are at a disadvantage in terms of family income compared to those with married parents. In the year 2000, only 14.6 percent of cohabiting men earned more than $50,000, compared to 27 percent of married men, reported Pamela Smock and Wendy Manning. Only 6 percent of husbands had earnings of less than $10,000, compared to 12 percent of cohabiting men. Cohabiting men are twice as likely as married men to be unemployed.

Educational Disadvantage

Statistically, children of unwed parents are born into homes with less-educated parents, which in turn handicaps them. They do less well in school than their peers living in married, two-biological-parent families. Adolescents with unmarried cohabiting parents are more likely than even their peers in single-mother households to be suspended or expelled.[21]

More Turmoil at Home

The most significant problem is that children of unwed parents suffer from a constant change in family structure. Half of such children— those over age twelve—live predominantly with one biological parent (usually the mother) *and that parent's live-in lover.* Many have already experienced a divorce and the loss of a father. Since the average cohabiting relationship lasts only 1.3 years, most children will experience the departure of at least a second male figure, and this is likely to develop into a pattern. The instability generates higher levels of depression in both the cohabiting adults and the children. Each change increases the likelihood that the child will fare poorly both emotionally and academically, including exhibiting behavioral problems.[22]

ECONOMIC HARDSHIP

People who cohabit are less likely to become affluent than those who marry. In 1975, married couples with children earned $56,102 on average. Even after adjusting for inflation, such couples were earning $89,045 in 2005. That's a healthy 59 percent income hike. By comparison, all households with children were earning $44,065 in 1975, but only $63,344 in 2005. That's only a 44 percent increase.[23] Marriage generates wealth; cohabitation does not.

Why?

Married couples pool their economic resources and have mutual financial goals that they sacrifice for and invest in. Cohabitors, in sharp contrast, usually keep separate bank accounts and do not plan for an economic future together, since he or she could walk out tomorrow. They tend to spend more on themselves, on such things as clothes and cars, which *depreciate,* rather than on a house, which *appreciates.*

The percentage of all households of married couples with children has fallen from 34.5 percent in 1975 to 23.7 percent. For the first time, less than a quarter of all households involve married couples, the lowest ever recorded by the U.S. Census.

RISK OF INFIDELITY

Over time, only 60 percent of cohabiting women are sexually faithful, compared to 90 percent of married women, according to a study in *Sexual Attitudes and Lifestyles*.

The National Sex Survey, based on detailed interviews with 3,500 American adults in 1992, conducted by Edward Laumann and colleagues at the University of Chicago, reported that 16 percent of cohabiting men said they had been unfaithful to their partners over the past year, versus only 4 percent of married men. Thus, cohabiting men were about *four times* as likely as husbands to report infidelity in the past year. In that same study, only 1 percent of married women committed adultery in the previous year, compared to 8 percent of cohabiting women. Women living with a man are *eight times* more likely than wives to cheat on their partners.[24]

Why does cohabitation involve so much infidelity?

A 2003 Gallup Poll found that cohabiting couples are twice as likely as married couples to view adultery as acceptable.

"People who are living with someone are keeping their options open, particularly if they are not engaged," wrote Linda Waite and

Maggie Gallagher.[25] For many cohabiting couples, living together is an extension of dating, which they believe entitles them to explore other options. Cohabitation is not full commitment—even if they are engaged, even if they have bought a house together. Cohabitors often lose respect for their partner and start looking over their shoulder for someone new. That little cloud of suspicion on the horizon can quickly grow into a dark thundercloud of infidelity.

HIGH RISK OF DIVORCE

If a cohabiting couple does marry, the problems unique to cohabitation are likely to be carried into their marriage. Newlyweds who lived together first are less happy or satisfied in their marriage than those who never lived together.[26] Dr. Joyce Brothers put it bluntly: "Cohabitation has a negative effect on the quality of a subsequent marriage."

For example, mature married love is built on the security of knowing that your spouse is sexually exclusive—that he or she is not physically intimate with anyone else. However, in the case of cohabitors who later wed, the tendency to be unfaithful is brought from the cohabiting relationship into the marriage. What's more, infidelity is a problem for both genders. If a couple lives together before marriage, either partner is more likely to cheat on the other after marriage.

That's why Dr. Laura Schlessinger, host of the nationally syndicated radio show *Dr. Laura*, scolds those who are "living together with your honey." In her book *Ten Stupid Things Women Do to Mess Up Their Lives,* she includes cohabiting as one of the top ten. "Dating—not living in—is supposed to be about learning and discerning" about a prospective mate.[27]

CHAPTER 3

LEGAL ENTANGLEMENTS
AND RISKS OF LIVING TOGETHER

The May 29, 2005, edition of the *Washington Post* featured, at the top of page 1, a photograph of twenty-three-month-old Colin Lovell being presented with an American flag during the funeral of his father, Gunnery Sgt. Barry Baker, at Arlington National Cemetery. The flag is traditionally given to the widow of a fallen soldier, not to his child. But Lael Lovell, Colin's mother, was not Sgt. Baker's widow. She was his girlfriend. Although the death of Sgt. Baker was a tragic event for his parents, his girlfriend, and his son, Ms. Lovell was denied far more than the flag upon the death of the twenty-four-year-old warrior. She was not eligible for his insurance benefits or widow's pension. Nor does her son carry his father's name. Everyone lost as a result of the young couple's decision to live together and have a child outside of marriage.

Colin Lovell's story is only one example of the legal risks of flouting the institution of marriage. Couples who cohabit often pay a high legal price, both while living together and when they break up.

Risks While Cohabiting

Financial, Medical, and Life-and-Death Decisions

Without a Durable Power of Attorney, cohabiting couples cannot make financial decisions for each other if injured or incapacitated. Nor can they make decisions about health care, end-of-life dilemmas, or funeral arrangements. Finally, cohabitors do not automatically receive survivor inheritance or Social Security without a will, living trust, or joint-tenancy agreement.

A number of these matters can be agreed upon by the couple in a

Domestic Partnership Agreement. Courts used to refuse to enforce Domestic Partnership Agreements that provided for property rights upon death or dissolution—"because they viewed them as a subterfuge for prostitution," according to Bethesda, Maryland, attorney Linda Ravdin. However, "as societal attitudes have changed, courts in the majority of states have held that a domestic partnership contract is enforceable if it meets the basic standards for validity of any contract."[28]

Marvin v. Marvin was a landmark 1977 case involving actor Lee Marvin and his live-in lover (who had taken his name). In it, the court recognized the right of unmarried cohabitors to enter into a contract to pool resources in which nonmonetary contributions to the family could be recognized as consideration for the acquisition of property and support rights. To date, at least thirty-nine states and the District of Columbia have approved enforcement of Domestic Partnership Agreements.[29]

This means that cohabiting couples have the right to make contracts; but the right to a fifty-fifty share of a house in the case of a breakup, for example, is not automatic, as it is in a legal marriage.

Very few cohabiting couples take legal steps to protect themselves. According to a survey of 1,380 cohabitors conducted by cohabiting .org, only 13.4 percent have a will, a mere 10 percent have "Joint Tenants with Rights of Survivorship," and 7 percent have a Durable Power of Attorney for health directives. Fully nine out of ten cohabitors are at serious legal risk.[30]

COMPLEX LEGAL ISSUES

Even if both parties are willing to enter into a legal agreement, the process can be extraordinarily complex. The March 19, 2005, *Washington Post* published a column by Benny L. Kass in response to this question from a reader:

I have a standard mortgage on a single-family house that I own by myself. I would like to add my live-in girlfriend to the deed. She will pay me half the current value of the house. If I do this, can I retain my current mortgage, thereby avoiding more closing costs and the loss of my favorable mortgage rate? Also, is this a taxable event that would require me to pay capital gains tax? I know that the simplest solution would be for us to get married, but there are other financial issues involved and we would like to avoid marriage now if possible.

Here is Mr. Kass's answer, which is remarkably complex, bristling with issues that couples living together never consider. He begins by agreeing with the writer that the best answer is to get married. However, since that option was off the table, Kass advised the writer that he had several legal issues to consider:

> **Your mortgage:** Let's assume that you purchased your home for $200,000 and that it is now worth $300,000. Your mortgage is $175,000. If your girlfriend is going to pay you half the value of the house, is she going to give you $150,000 in cash (half of $300,000)? Or is she going to pay you $62,500, the difference between half of the current value of the house and half of the mortgage debt—that is, is she buying half of your equity ($150,000 minus $87,500 equals $62,500)?
>
> Do you plan to take all of the mortgage interest tax deductions on your own, or will they be divided equally? If your girlfriend wants those tax deductions, she will have to be added to the deed of trust (the mortgage) that you have with your lender . . .

Tax consequences: Again, assume you paid $200,000 for the house and it's worth $300,000 now. If you sell half the property to your girlfriend, you will make a profit of $50,000.

Mr. Kass asked:

> What happens if one of you dies? Do you want your girlfriend to inherit the entire property, in which case title should be held as joint tenants with rights of survivorship? Or do you want your heirs and relatives to get the property, in which case title should be held as tenants in common?
>
> What happens if one of you decides to end the relationship? What will happen to the house? Who will pay the mortgage? What if one of you is unable to make the monthly payments? What about furniture? Who owns it? How will it be disposed of should you split up?

Columnist Kass knows there is a strong likelihood that the couple will split up because he closes by suggesting they enter into a legal arrangement now "while you are still friendly" rather than try to resolve the issues later with lawyers ("when you are not talking").

Risks While Separating

This is the title of a brief chapter in *How You Can Avoid Legal Land Mines,* by Joseph S. Lyles, an attorney in Greenville, South Carolina. He noted that if you live with someone without the legal status of marriage, the biggest problem "is presented when it falls apart."[31]

No Legal Property Ownership Rights

Jan lived with a man for two years, during which they opened a bar and she worked without pay for a year. "She helped renovate the building before the business even opened. When the business started running smoothly, Jan's significant other ended the relationship," Lyles reported.

Her significant other owned the house in which they lived. Jan's name was not on the lease of the building where the bar operated. She was not even listed as the owner of one of their two cars. "Jan was unmarried and therefore could not file a divorce action and demand a fair share of the marital property. *Without a marriage, there was no marital property to divide* and there was no paper trail to document her contributions to the business venture" (emphasis added).

Harriet and I met a woman who told us, "I have been living with a man for six years. The relationship is over, and I want to move out. He says, 'Go ahead.' But he won't give me the mortgage payments I have made over the years, explaining that he doesn't have the money. He also refuses to put our house up for sale so I can recoup my investment."

Had she married the man and divorced him, she would have had a legal right to half of the house's value. As a cohabitor, however, she has no clear legal rights. What likely lies ahead for her is a long, costly legal battle.

Cohabitors who buy property together ought to have a legal agreement that clarifies how much each party owns and includes a title such as "Joint Tenants with Rights of Survivorship," meaning that if one partner dies, the other automatically inherits the whole house. The couple also should have a written agreement regarding the house in the event the couple breaks up. Will one person have the first right to stay in the house, perhaps to care for a child, and buy the other out? Or will the house be sold and the proceeds divided? What are the buy-out rights?

A woman wrote this plaintive e-mail to cohabiting.org:

> I have been living with someone for almost 10 years, and he wants me to leave his house. I want to take everything, but he says it's his. He furnished the house, saying that it was "our" bedroom set, "our" everything. And I told him that, and he says it's not in writing. What can I do?[32]

Like this woman, many individuals who have cohabited are bereft when the relationship ends. What one partner perceives as an understanding that both share ownership of possessions can be ignored later by the other partner. Millions of live-in partners—mostly women—are in legal limbo. It's one of the biggest risks of cohabitation. When the relationship ends, which is likely, both partners can find themselves in economic purgatory. They're stuck. One partner is unable to recoup funds invested unless the other person agrees. The law that exists to protect citizens cannot be enforced if there is no contract of a binding union. If both names are on the deed, there is more hope, but if one partner is unwilling to sell, costly legal action is needed to force the sale of the home before both can extract their investment.

Misunderstandings About Common-Law Marriage

Many partners who have lived together for several years think they have a legal common-law marriage. If a relationship dissolves, each may assume he or she has 50 percent ownership of any shared assets. However, few cohabiting couples' relationships qualify as legal common-law marriages. Common-law marriages are recognized in *only fourteen states*—Alabama, Colorado, Georgia, Idaho (if the common-law status was created before January 1, 1996), Kansas, Montana, New Hampshire (for inheritance purposes only), Ohio (if created before October 10, 1991), Oklahoma, Pennsylvania, Rhode Island, South Carolina, Texas, and Utah—and the District of Columbia.

Even then, a couple does not have a common-law marriage unless (1) they intend to be married; (2) they use the same last name; (3) they file a joint tax return; and (4) they live together in one of the states (or the District of Columbia) for a significant amount of time (which is not specified).

Michelle wrote to cohabiting.org:

> I have lived with and been devoted to a man for 6 years. We now share the same last name but have recently gone our separate ways with no chance of reconciliation. In my understanding we are considered common-law married. I need some advice as to whether I need to file for a divorce.[33]

Sadly, this woman is confused. Since she is not married, she can't file for divorce. She thinks she has a common-law marriage. But odds are she doesn't meet the criteria. Had she been married, she would have had a legal right to half of their home's value. Now she is in legal limbo and may lose all the money she paid toward the mortgage. More important, she's lost six years of her life. She's now older, and is unlikely to be able to afford a lawyer to sue to recoup her investment.

Child Custody Disputes

Cohabitors also have no clear guidelines regarding access to their children should they separate. Custody and visitation issues divorcing couples face are compounded for unmarried couples by the lack of definitive rules regarding cohabitation. However, one thing is clear: if a man fathers a child, he is legally responsible for paying child support until the child reaches age eighteen. Even if the couple is divorced and the man is affluent, he is very unlikely to continue support past eighteen, and less than 30 percent will pay college tuition.[34]

THE LEGAL ALTERNATIVE: MARRIAGE

A simple alternative to these legal difficulties does exist: marriage. It provides protection to both spouses and to their children. If a couple divorces, they generally have a right to share in the value of a house, for example, on a fifty-fifty basis—even if only one spouse earned the money to pay the mortgage. If a man and woman enter a marriage with unequal assets—unless there is a prenuptial agreement in which both parties have consulted a lawyer and both agree in advance that some of the couple's assets will be split unequally in the case of divorce—those assets generally are to be divided equitably between the man and the woman. Even the income-earning partner's future retirement benefits are to be shared. Conversely, if one spouse files for divorce and obtains custody of the children, he or she must give the child's other parent access to their children (except in special cases).

Marriage is the only institution that provides true protection for both parties.

The Unpleasant Truth About Cohabitation

There is a time for everything, and a season for every activity under heaven: . . . a time to embrace and a time to refrain.

Ecclesiastes 3:1, 5

Cohabitation—it's training for divorce.

Charles Colson

A S CHILDREN WE sang a nursery rhyme:

> Bob and Bettie sitting in a tree
> K-I-S-S-I-N-G
> First comes love,
> Then comes marriage,
> Then comes baby in a baby carriage.

But the rampantly growing pattern of couples living together has profoundly, insidiously, and negatively transformed our culture. For hundreds of years in America, the natural order of relationships was a set, prescribed sequence: first love, then marriage, and then a baby. No longer. The sequence of events has been turned on its head—with tragic consequences. Now:

> First comes sex,
> Then comes living together,

Then comes pregnancy,
Then comes abortion or a baby,
Then half split
While some marry.
Of those who do,
Two-thirds divorce.

Almost imperceptibly America has moved from a culture of marriage to a culture of cohabitation. Without debate or public notice, and with too little dismay or concern voiced even by the church, living together has become the dominant way American couples start their life together.

Michael Douglas and Catherine Zeta-Jones were pictured happily cuddling their two-week-old son, Dylan, on the cover of *US Weekly* in the summer of 2000. The then-fifty-five-year-old Douglas was enthusiastic about his thirty-year-old companion: "Love is something that's so rewarding. It just makes you feel great to have something to cherish, something to protect, something to nurture," he gushed.

When asked about the values she wanted to instill in baby Dylan, Zeta-Jones replied, "I just want him to be a good solid boy, knowing right from wrong. I'm already dreaming of his getting married. I'm having these vivid dreams of me and Michael standing in the church, and he's squeezing my hand."

Presumably the couple read their own comments and concluded that they should marry if their child was to learn right from wrong and if they were to realize their dreams of attending his wedding. Three months later they tied the knot in a million-dollar wedding.

Unfortunately, this celebrity couple is not unique. According to a Gallup Poll, the proportion of married Americans who live together before tying the knot has steadily increased. When Gallup first asked about cohabitation in 1988, only 19 percent had cohabited prior to their wedding; but that figure nearly doubled, to 37 percent, by 2002.[1]

Gallup estimates a majority (51 percent) of married people under age fifty report that they lived together before marrying. Scholars now estimate that up to two-thirds of weddings in 2007 are preceded by cohabitation. That's one major reason divorce rates have hung at such high levels despite the 50 percent plunge in marriage rates.

A HARD LOOK AT COHABITATION

Cohabitation, as defined by *Webster's Collegiate Dictionary,* is "to live together as husband and wife usually without legal or religious sanction." Forty years ago, our parents' generation called it "shacking up" or "living in sin." However, as the pattern has grown, contemporary culture has become more accepting and has sanitized our language with such politically correct terms as "living together" or "trial marriage." Academicians call it "cohabitation."

Today young couples tend to view living together as extended dating. By high-school graduation 47 percent of students have had sexual intercourse. As recently as the late 1960s, more than 40 percent of women were virgins when they married. Now the figure is about 10 percent. Coed college dorms have all but destroyed natural modesty, and "hooking up" is the norm for millions of students.[2] The next barrier to fall was the genders living separately. Not even clergy call cohabitation "living in sin" anymore. Our culture accepts living together as the new norm.

Cohabiting couples embark on their journey with the same bright hope as those directly entering marriage. Few anticipate the havoc and pain this altered style of dating can create. For most, catastrophe awaits.

- Only two out of ten cohabiting couples are able to build a lasting marriage.

- Nearly half of cohabiting couples break up before the wedding. Their "premarital divorce" frequently is no less painful than divorce itself.
- Those cohabiting couples who do marry are 50 percent more likely to divorce than those who had never lived together.

"Trying on the shoe before you buy it" seems logical. The trouble is, the cohabitation shoe rarely fits. Tens of millions of couples have broken up either before or after the wedding. Abandoned partners often try living with another partner, but those relationships tend to last an even shorter time. Serial cohabitation can become a pattern. In the search for the perfect partner, the "soul mate," what's lost in the shuffle is marriage itself, the original goal. Some, however, do learn the lesson. In a January 16, 2007, article in the *New York Times,* Emily Zuzik, thirty-two, gave her reaction to living with two boyfriends: "I don't plan to live with anyone else again until I am married."

WHY LIVING TOGETHER CAN SEEM LIKE A GOOD IDEA

Cohabitation is a halfway house for people who don't want the degree of personal and social commitment required by marriage, at least for now.[3] According to participants who have written to cohabiting.org, the website about cohabiting couples, some of the perceived benefits of living together include:

- The convenience of sex being "readily available";
- Being able to share responsibility for "rent, cooking, etc.";
- Independence—keeping "money separate";

- The ability to "avoid responsibility of partner's debts";
- The presumption that leaving is easy "if things get too rough";
- The hope that they'll be able to "avoid pain and stigma of divorce";
- "More individual free time";
- The freedom of having "no obligation to care for partner or their children if sick, lose their job or unable to care for themselves";
- Believing that there are "no sexual strings attached";
- Feeling "free to see others";
- Being entitled to "love 'em and leave 'em";
- Having "no legal entanglements";
- "No nagging"; and
- Not feeling overly invested in the relationship: "easy come, easy go."[4]

Cohabitation does appear to offer some short-term advantages:

- Individuals can keep their money separate and avoid responsibility for their partner's debts.
- A person whose marriage has failed may be skittish about remarriage but can easily find someone willing to cohabit.
- A retired man and woman who are both widowed may move in together, forgoing marriage, because they don't want their Social Security benefits to be reduced.

In just two generations the number of cohabiting couples has sky-rocketed, from 439,000 to 5.4 million (not including gay couples). That's a *twelvefold* increase. Furthermore, this number only represents couples cohabiting in a given month. Over the course of a year, the numbers may be 8 to 10 million. By contrast, only 2.23 million marriages were recorded in 2005.[5] Thus, more than twice as many couples are living together outside of wedlock at any moment as marry in a whole year.

To put it differently, the percentage of marriages preceded by cohabitation jumped from about 10 percent for those marrying between 1965 and 1974 to "41 percent among the 1980–84 marriage cohort, to 56 percent for marriages ten years later."[6]

Increase of Cohabiting Couples

Year	Number of Cohabiting Couples
1960	439,000
1970	523,000
1980	1,589,000
1990	2,856,000
2000	4,736,000
2005	5,186,000[7]
2006	5,368,000

To anyone over age fifty, these trends are shocking. Yet cohabitation makes eminent sense to young people. When high-school students were asked if they agree with the proposition "that most people will have fuller and happier lives if they choose legal marriage rather than staying single or just living with someone," less than a third of girls (32 percent) and only 37.5 percent of boys agreed![8]

The kids could not be more wrong. Cohabitation has tragic consequences for millions of adults hoping to find true, lasting love.

CONSEQUENCES OF COHABITATION

Cohabiting Couples Tend to Be Younger

According to the U.S. Census Bureau, 24 percent of cohabiting women and 16 percent of cohabiting men were under age twenty-five. By contrast, only 4 percent of married women and 2 percent of married men were this young when they married. About a third of all men and women aged twenty-five to thirty-four are unmarried partners.[9]

The National Survey of Families and Households, conducted by Dr. Bumpass and colleagues, is a major source of information about cohabiting couples. The survey found that the number of marriages preceded by cohabitation rose from about 10 percent for those married between 1965 to 1974 to more than 50 percent for those marrying between 1990 and 1994, and the percentage is higher for remarriages. The percentage of women in their late thirties who have cohabited jumped from 30 percent in 1987 to 48 percent in 1995.

Dr. Bumpass now estimates that a quarter of unmarried American women aged twenty-five to thirty-nine are currently living with a partner, and another quarter have done so in the past. His newest estimate is that 58 percent of those who marry were already living together, versus virtually none fifty years ago.[10]

Cohabitors Tend to Be Less Educated

Of women aged nineteen to forty-four, nearly 60 percent of high-school dropouts have lived with a man, while less than 40 percent of those with a college education have done so. About 30 percent of husbands and 25 percent of wives were college graduates in 2000, but only 18 percent and 17 percent of cohabiting men and women.[11]

Cohabitors Tend to Have Lower Incomes

Cohabitation for some is a "poor man's marriage." Cohabiting men are twice as likely as married men to be unemployed. According to a report by Pamela Smock and Wendy Manning, in the year 2000, only 14.6 percent of cohabiting men earned over $50,000, compared to 27 percent of married men. Only 6 percent of husbands had earnings of less than $10,000, compared to 12 percent of cohabiting men.

Cohabitors Tend to Be More Liberal

Adult children of divorce whose mothers expressed more approval of living together were more likely to cohabit themselves. They are more prone to risk than noncohabitors. "Cohabitors profess somewhat more liberal gender-role attitudes than do married couples," writes Pamela Smock.[12] Such people are "more gender-egalitarian" than married counterparts, more likely to eschew the traditional male breadwinner role and embrace an equal economic responsibility.

Cohabitors Tend to Be Less Religious

More than half of cohabitors say they are atheists. All are less likely to be church members or to attend church services.

Cohabitors Tend to Be Less Committed

Those who live together are less committed to marriage as an institution and are more accepting of divorce. They tend to view cohabitation as extended dating and are less likely to be sexually exclusive. Yet they parrot the myth, "We're in a committed relationship."

Cohabitors Tend to Be More Selfish

Cohabitors place more emphasis on independence and economic equality than couples who don't live together. In contrast, married couples are likely to share resources and value interdependence.

Four Types of Cohabiting Couples

1. *Prenuptial:* Some couples who live together are engaged and plan to live together for a brief period to save money before their wedding. Relatively few couples fit this category.
2. *Testing the relationship:* Far more common are couples who say they are testing their compatibility for marriage. These often are children of divorce who fear marriage.
3. *Sequel to a failed marriage:* After divorce, a high percentage of people with children will cohabit with a partner, according to Ron Deal, author of *The Smart Stepfamily*.
4. *Escaping a bad family situation:* A few women move in with a boyfriend to escape a dysfunctional home, a particularly unhealthy reason to do so—leaving one dysfunctional home for another.

Is it any wonder that people who cohabit are less happy, less healthy, less wealthy, die younger, and have less gratifying sex than married couples do?

A Double Cancer of Marriage

Cohabitation kills marriages at two stages. *First, it is an invisible cancer at the front end,* diverting tens of millions from getting married at all. Second, *cohabitation is a deadly cancer at the center of marriage.* Couples who live together are 50 percent more likely to divorce than those who never cohabited, according to Dr. Larry Bumpass of the University of Wisconsin. Let's explore both deadly killers in more detail.

The Marriage Rate Has Plunged in Half

Many know that half of America's marriages end in divorce. What few realize is that *the marriage rate has plummeted more than 50 percent since 1970,* according to the National Marriage Project at Rutgers University. Census reports that in 1970, there were 76.5 marriages per 1,000 women. By 2005 that fell to only 38.7 marriages per 1,000. That is a 50.7 percent drop. Why has the marriage rate plunged in half? The culprit is living together, the single greatest threat to the institution of marriage in America. The sad fact is that the percentage of never-married Americans between ages 30 and 44 has tripled from 6.8 percent in 1970 to 20.4 percent in 2005. In fact, a higher percentage of couples are cohabiting in Canada and Europe, and their marriage rates have fallen more than in the U.S. These statistics bear out the disturbing truth that millions who begin living together, thinking it is a step toward marriage, have inadvertently substituted cohabitation for marriage.

Millions of Cohabitors Never Marry

Contrary to what they may think, couples who decide to live together are not postponing making a decision about marriage but are actually making a decision *not* to marry. Cohabiting is not a way to prepare for marriage but a way to prolong singleness. Most cohabiting couples break up in a year or so. According to R. R. Rindfuss and A. Vanden-heuvel, "Cohabiting couples . . . do not want to be committed. They want it where they can get out pretty easy if they want to. Easy to walk out the door." The authors make a persuasive case that those who live together more closely resemble single people than a married couple.[13]

- They keep their money separate rather than having joint bank accounts.
- Most do not buy property together or list one another as beneficiaries on insurance policies.

A couple we know has three daughters, ages thirty-five to forty, all of whom have cohabited; none has married. This is by no means an unusual situation today. Cohabitation has diverted millions of people from *ever* getting married. The percentage of never-married singles aged thirty to forty-four tripled from 8 percent for men in 1970 to 23.8 percent in 2005, and for women from 5.6 percent to 17 percent.[14] The actual numbers of never-married men and women in that age group jumped from 2,329,000 to 12,865,000—*more than 550 percent.* When you include never-married people aged eighteen and older, the number increases to 52 million!

Never-Married People Aged Thirty to Forty-four

	1970		2005	
	Number	%	Number	%
Men	1,348,000	8.0	7,462,000	23.8
Women	981,000	5.6	5,403,000	17.0
Totals	2,329,000	6.8	12,865,000	20.4

Most of these unmarried Americans have not remained chaste. Nor are they merely sexually active. Larry L. Bumpass, Ph.D., James A. Sweet, Ph.D., and Andrew Cherlin, Ph.D., write in a 1995 paper to the Population Association of America, "By now about half of the population under age 40 have lived with an unmarried partner—in ten years that will be true for the population under age 50."[15]

Their prediction was wrong. As the Gallup Poll reported in 2002, that landmark was achieved in just seven years.[16] For millions, living together has become an acceptable alternative to marriage.

Cohabitors Who Marry Are 50 Percent More Likely to Divorce

Living together is a trap. A comprehensive National Survey of Families and Households conducted interviews of 13,000 people in 1987–1988 and concluded that while 40 percent of couples who live together will break up before marriage and another 10 percent will continue living together without marrying, 50 percent do eventually marry.[17] But even for the half who marry, the outlook is grim: "Marriages that are preceded by living together have 50% higher disruption rates than marriages without premarital cohabitation."

What exactly does this statistic mean? The divorce rate for first marriages is 45 percent. Therefore, instead of 45 percent of every fifty cohabiting couples who marry divorcing (twenty-two couples), half again as many will do so (thirty-three couples)—two-thirds will divorce. When added to the forty-five couples who break up short of marriage, that's an abysmal failure rate of seventy-eight out of one hundred "trial marriages." This does not count the ten couples who are still cohabiting after five years, another eight of whom will likely fail, bringing the total failure rate to eighty-six of the original one hundred couples!

This math is conservative and is based on first marriages; yet many cohabitations follow a failed marriage. Second marriages fail at a 60 percent rate; 70 percent if stepchildren are involved, according to E. Mavis Hetherington.[18] Therefore, only ten to twenty of the original one hundred premarital cohabiting couples can expect to have marriages lasting ten years or more. Why would anyone want to risk entering into a relationship with an 80 percent or higher likelihood of failure?

Sadly, most couples do not *know* their risks of failure. Our culture bombards us with the message that practically everyone is living with someone outside of marriage. Little attention is focused on the truth that living together can be a dead end.

No group is more supportive of living together—despite evidence that four out of five couples who begin cohabiting will not build a lasting marriage—than the young. While 90 percent of teenagers believe in marriage, they view cohabitation as a stepping-stone in the relationship—a good way to get know their partner and avoid a future divorce. Sixty-nine percent say they "approve" of couples "living together before they get married."[19] They say, "If things don't work out, we can chalk it up to experience and move on. At least we will have learned something about ourselves and marriage."[20]

Pamela Smock, Ph.D., a sociologist at the University of Michigan, writes: "Common sense suggests that premarital cohabitation should provide an opportunity for couples to learn about each other, strengthen their bonds, and increase their chances for a successful marriage. . . . The evidence, however, suggests just the opposite. Premarital cohabitation tends to be associated with lower marital quality and to increase the risk of divorce, even after taking into account of variables known to be associated with divorce. . . . The degree of consensus about this central finding is impressive."[21]

What starts as lower levels of commitment among those who choose to cohabit eventually translates into lower levels of relationship happiness both before and after the wedding, if there is a wedding.

This outcome will come as a surprise to men who insist on living with a woman before considering marriage. The truth is, instead of improving their odds of success, they unwittingly improve their odds of *failure*.

Why is the divorce rate so much higher for couples who marry after cohabiting? Two theories have credence.

I. THE "SELECTION EFFECT"

The first theory, put forth by Dr. Bumpass, is the "selection effect." Those who live together before marriage differ substantially from those who do not, and those differences increase the likelihood of marital instability for former cohabitors.

Cohabitors tend to be less educated. For example, cohabiting women are twice as likely to be high-school dropouts than college graduates. Cohabitors also tend to have nontraditional values and attitudes. They are less likely to be religious and more likely to dismiss advice to remain chaste before marriage. They are more likely to be children of divorce. They are less committed to marriage and, when troubles arise, more open to divorce.

The problem with this theory is that most high-school dropouts in 1960 didn't cohabit before they married, nor did the less religious nor the more liberal. It simply *was not done*. Additionally, few of their parents had divorced.

What has changed the culture so dramatically? The Sexual Revolution. When the birth control pill was introduced, the perceived dangers of premarital sex were lessened and the era of "free love" was ushered in. Premarital sexual activity brought less of a stigma; it actually became a badge of honor and a sign of modernity. Eventually sex without the bonds of marriage became accepted as the norm. The "*Playboy* Philosophy," popularized by Hugh Hefner, promoted consensual sex anywhere, anytime, with anyone. Widespread cohabitation is the logical outgrowth of such a societal frame of reference.

2. THE COHABITATION EFFECT

The other, more probable, theory to explain why living together dooms so many marriages is that the experience of cohabiting changes young adults in ways that increase their chances of divorce. The very act of cohabiting, with its casual, impermanent bonding, diminishes respect for commitment, especially the till-death-do-us-part vows of marriage.

As Pamela Smock notes: "Through cohabitation people learn about and come to accept the temporary nature of relationships and in particular that there are alternatives to marriage." She cites a study showing that living together between the ages of eighteen and twenty-three "significantly alters young men's and women's attitudes toward marriage and divorce." It changes "people's attitudes in ways that make them more prone to divorce."[22]

But cohabitation changes even more than people's perspectives on marriage and divorce. It seems to dramatically affect the way people view and respond to their partners. Dr. Catherine Cohan of Pennsylvania State University explained to Reuters Health what she observed in yet another eye-opening study comparing the marriages of people who had cohabited with those who had not: "Those people who lived together were more negative and less positive when resolving a marital problem and when providing support to their partner." She found that even those who cohabited for *just one month* before marriage actually displayed poorer communication and problem-solving skills than those who did not live together.

According to Dr. Cohan's report, coauthored with Stacey Kleinbaum, in the February 2002 issue of the *Journal of Marriage and Family,* 60 percent of test subjects who had cohabited before marriage were more verbally aggressive, less supportive of one another, and more hostile than the 40 percent of spouses who had not lived together.

Researchers visited the couples at home, interviewed partners separately, and then videotaped two fifteen-minute sessions, in the absence of the interviewer, in which the partners sought to solve a problem that had been selected by each from a list that included sex, money, children, housework, career, and religion. The videotapes revealed that couples who had first lived together displayed more negative behavior than those who had not. Husbands who had cohabited, for example, were more likely to attempt to control their wives, while the wives were more verbally aggressive.

Cohan and Kleinbaum concluded that couples who live together before marriage enter the relationship with lower commitment. It takes a higher level of commitment to marry than to cohabit. "The open-ended nature of the relationship may cause them to be less motivated to develop their conflict resolution and support skills."

The researchers said those who cohabited were not doomed to divorce but did have "poorer communication skills" than those who remained separate until the wedding. Cohan added, "I can say, however, there's nothing in the research that says living together helps people in the long run."

People who cohabit seem to lose respect for themselves and for their partner, while those who form a household only after marriage have inherently higher self-respect and respect for their spouse.

Cohabitation is a supercharged engine producing dissatisfied couples and, as a result, more divorces—thus contributing to and sustaining America's high divorce rate.

LEARNING FROM THE PAST, GUARDING THE FUTURE

A Lesson from Ancient Rome

The concept of a trial marriage is not a revolutionary, modern idea that originated in the 1960s. It actually dates back two thousand years, to the Roman system of a one-year trial marriage known as the *usus* marriage. According to Dr. Paul Pearsall, author of *Ten Laws of Lasting Love*, it was the lowest of three levels of marriage in ancient Rome.

The highest level of marriage commitment—the most desirable level—was called the *confarreatio*. Pearsall explained that it was

> highly ceremonious and almost impossible to end by any legal or socially approved means. The welfare of the Roman society and cultural system came first over all else, and High Monogamy was supposed to be strong enough to survive for the general welfare of everyone else. As the Roman citizen was expected to put the state above all else, spouses in the *confarreatio* marriage were expected to place their own needs below the welfare of the marital union. The Romans saw marital survival and not individual assertiveness as the sign of personal maturity and responsibility.
>
> The next level of marriage was the *coemptio* union, in which the Romans had little faith. After a brief legal ceremony, the bride was given to the groom to "use" as he wished for cooking, cleaning, and sex. In trade, the wife received financial support and security. This form of "very low monogamy" was tolerated but never admired or advocated by the Romans. . . .
>
> Finally, the Roman system of marriage included the *usus,* or "trial marriage" for one year. If the couple qualified after that year, they could decide to try for the High Monogamy of the *confarreatio* marriage. The *usus* marriage was one of the earliest institutionalized arrangements for cohabitation.[23]

Similar to today, when cohabitation rarely leads to a joyous, lasting marriage, "the *usus* marriage failed the Romans because only a small percentage of these marriages survived the one-year trial period."[24]

Why? Pearsall explained: "High Monogamy requires a promise of commitment to join forever. The idea of 'trying it for a while first' negates the very basis of the Great Marriage Myth."[25]

As the ancient Roman culture gave way to Christianity in the third century, only the High Monogamy model of marriage was honored and considered legal. The *usus* marriage (trial marriage) failed nearly 1,700 years ago. Americans could learn from history.

In fact, for a time America did learn this lesson. Until 1970 cohabitation was illegal in every state. In 2002 it was still illegal in eight states.

A Warning from Modern Europe

Europe has traveled even farther down the cohabitation path than has America, giving us a unique opportunity to see where we're heading if we don't correct our course. The relationship of falling marriage rates to rising cohabitation rates is even more pronounced in Europe than in the United States. Cohabitation rates are higher in Europe than they are in America. Scandinavia, frequently called the "California of Europe," is often a negative trendsetter. Consider these portents:

- In Scandinavia, cohabitation rates tripled in just a decade (from 1987 to 1997).
- Cohabitation is more common than marriage for Scandinavians under age thirty. One consequence of this trend away from marriage is that more than half of babies are born to unwed mothers in Sweden (54 percent) and Iceland (an eye-popping 65 percent) and

nearly half in Norway (49 percent) and Denmark (46 percent). These figures are twice the percentage of continental Europe and nearly 60 percent higher than in the United States.

- Scandinavia's marriage rate has plunged even more than America's. While 9 people per 1,000 married per year in the 1950s, that ratio plummeted to just 4 per 1,000 in the 1990s. That's a 55 percent plunge in the marriage rate.

- In England 70 percent of women currently cohabit before marriage, compared to only 5 percent in the mid-1960s.[26]

Is this grim picture of Scandinavia and Britain predicting America's future? Unless millions of Americans change their minds and decide *not* to live together, the answer is yes. Our marriage rates are steadily decreasing and already are only half of what they were in 1970.

As we've already seen, the falling marriage rate is closely linked to the rise in cohabitation. Living together is the single greatest threat to the institution of marriage in America—and around the world. Millions of couples are substituting cohabitation for marriage.

Cohabitation is a trap that can actually prevent those who aspire to marriage from achieving that goal. Our nation would have 1.1 million more marriages a year—3.3 million instead of 2.2 million—if the same percentage of couples who married in 1970 were marrying in 2008. If the current trend is not reversed, cohabitation might virtually replace marriage.

CHAPTER 5

A Case for Marriage

A wife of noble character who can find? She is worth far more than rubies. Her husband has full confidence in her and lacks nothing of value. She brings him good, not harm, all the days of her life.

Proverbs 31:10–12

Behold, the institution of marriage! It is one of the Creator's most marvelous and enduring gifts to humankind. . . . Five thousand years of recorded history have come and gone, yet every civilization in the history of the world has been built upon it. . . . The institution of marriage represents the very foundation of human social order. Everything of value sits on that base. Institutions, governments, religious fervor, and the welfare of children are all dependent on its stability. When it is weakened or undermined, the entire superstructure begins to wobble.

Dr. James Dobson, *Marriage Under Fire*

WHEN A 2002 Gallup Poll asked couples to grade their marriage on an A-to-F scale, the results were as follows:

A—68 percent
B—23 percent
C—6 percent
D—1 percent
F—1 percent[1]

Not a bad showing for marriage.

How would unmarried couples living together rate the quality of their relationships? We believe that half of cohabitors would give their relationships no more than a C—and many would grade them lower, a D or even an F. That's because marriage is the best way to live together. Singles need to plan for the real thing, marriage, and avoid the counterfeit of cohabitation.

As this book was going to press, we came across a survey that proves our gut assessment. Of 17,024 people preparing for marriage who took the PREPARE premarital inventory, nearly two-thirds (64 percent) of cohabiting couples ranked their relationships in the "low satisfaction group." By contrast, almost two-thirds (also 64 percent) of those living apart fell into the "very satisfied group," according to Dr. David Olson, president of Life Innovations, which created the PREPARE premarital inventory.[2]

Curiously, in spite of their own living arrangements, even couples who cohabit seem to intrinsically know that marriage is the best way to live together. Many may feel uneasy or even guilty about living with their partner without the blessing of marriage. In fact, in another cohabiting.org survey, 59 percent of cohabiting couples who responded said they believe cohabitation is wrong but continue living together anyway.[3]

Yet there is a way of living together that can succeed. It's an old-fashioned concept called *marriage*. Consider the practical value of marriage:

While cohabitors as a group are younger, less educated, less wealthy, more socially liberal, less religious, and more selfish, married couples tend to be happier, healthier, and wealthier than those who are not married. They also live longer and have more—and better—sex.

Additionally, marriage is the foundation for societal order, our culture's most important institution for fostering parental investment in children and for ensuring that men and women find a common life of mutual affection, care, and sexual intimacy.

In *The Case for Marriage: Why Married People Are Happier, Healthier and Better Off Financially,* Linda J. Waite and Maggie Gallagher detail and document the advantages of marriage. Their book cites numerous studies to back up the case for marriage and is a must-read for clergy, church leaders, and parents of single adult children immersed in the risky lifestyle of cohabitation.

Married Couples Are Happier

"Married men and women report less depression, less anxiety, and lower levels of other types of psychological distress than do those who are single, divorced, or widowed,"[4] Waite and Gallagher report.

They cite a study of fourteen thousand adults over a ten-year period that found that marital status was one of the most important predictors of happiness. Among the married, 40 percent said they were "very happy with their life in general, compared to just under a quarter of those who were single or who were cohabiting." Only 15 percent of those who were separated and 18 percent of those who were divorced claimed to be that happy. Furthermore, "married people were also about half as likely as singles or cohabitors to say they are unhappy with their lives."[5]

In citing results from another, even larger study (nearly twenty thousand people questioned over the last several decades), the authors confirm the case for greater personal happiness among married couples than among others. The studies showed that 66 percent of husbands and 62 percent of wives gave their marriage the highest possible happiness rating. "Almost no one—2 percent of the married men and 4 percent of the married women—described their marriage as 'not too happy.' "[6]

"Nor do unhappy marriages necessarily stay that way: 86 percent of those who rated their marriage as unhappy in the late eighties and who were still married five years later said their marriages had become happier,"[7] according to an analysis by Linda Waite of 5,232 married adults interviewed in the National Survey of Families and Households at the University of Chicago, which she reported as coauthor of *The Case for Marriage*. In the late 1980s, 645 spouses of the 5,232 rated their marriage as unhappy. Five years later, these same people were re-interviewed.

> Most say they have become very happy indeed. In fact, nearly three-fifths of those who said their marriage was unhappy in the late 80s and who stayed married rated that same marriage "very happy" or "quite happy" when re-interviewed five years later. Permanent marital unhappiness is surprisingly rare among the couples who stuck it out. Five years later just 15 percent of those who initially said they were very unhappily married, ranked their marriage as not unhappy at all.[8]

Remember that number—86 percent of bad marriages become good ones. The next time you hear a friend or relative suggest or threaten divorce, you might say, "You took a vow to remain together 'for better, for worse . . . till death do you part.' You're now in a 'worse' period that many marriages experience. But studies show it's likely to improve. So stick to your vows, pray, and trust the Lord. Marriage is a process, giving spouses a shared purpose that enhances their happiness."

As Waite and Gallagher put it: "Ordinary, good-enough marriages provide the partners with a sense that what they do matters, that someone cares for, esteems, needs, loves, and values them as a person. No matter what else happens in life, this knowledge makes problems easier to bear."[9]

And what of those who divorced? "Conventional wisdom would argue that unhappily married adults who divorced would be better off: happier, less depressed, with greater self-esteem," asserted a noted 2002 report based on the same study, "Does Divorce Make People Happy?"[10] The answer is *no*.

"Unhappily married adults who divorced or separated were no happier, on average, than unhappily married adults who stayed married. Divorce did not reduce symptoms of depression for unhappily married adults, or raise their self-esteem or increase their sense of mastery, on average." In fact, "unhappy marriages were less common than unhappy spouses," and 74 percent of them were happy five years earlier.

Moral: it pays to observe one's marriage vows—for better or for worse—because most bad marriages will get better, and opting out is no real help.

Married Couples Are Healthier

In a 1990 article for *Physician* magazine titled "Divorce: A Hazard to Your Health?" the late Dr. David Larson and his wife, Susan, wrote:

> In light of current research, the Surgeon General might consider warning married couples about the potential health and behavioral risks of divorce. Research studies show that divorce and the process of marital breakup puts people at much higher risk for both psychiatric and physical disease—even cancer. . . . Being divorced and a non-smoker is only slightly less dangerous than smoking a pack or more a day and staying married. . . . Every type of terminal cancer strikes divorced individuals of either sexes [sic], both white and non-white, more frequently than it does married people.[11]

The Larsons cited the research of James J. Lynch, author of *A Cry Unheard: New Insights into the Medical Consequences of Loneliness*, which reveals that in any given year, divorced men are twice as likely as married men to die from the four biggest killers: heart disease, stroke, hypertension, and cancer. Auto accidents and suicide death rates for the divorced are almost four times higher; cirrhosis of the liver and pneumonia death rates are seven times higher; the rate of death from murder is eight times greater; and psychiatric illness is ten times more likely for divorced men when compared with married men. The rates are similarly high for men who were widowed or single.[12]

Why? "Single men drink almost twice as much as married men of the same age," write Waite and Gallagher. "Nor is downing one too many the only way single men put their lives at risk. Single men are also more likely to smoke, to drink and drive, to drive too fast, to get into fights, and to take other risks that increase the chances of accidents and injuries."[13]

On the other hand, married men tend to settle down. According to a recent national survey, only one married man in seven says his drinking causes him problems at work or problems with aggression. By comparison, one in four single men of the same age says his drinking causes such problems. In fact, "only one out of six single guys drinks so little as to be a virtual abstainer, compared to one out of four married men."[14]

Divorce also impacts women's health, but to a lesser degree since they tend to be not as "wild" as single men. A study of twenty thousand white women between the ages of eighteen and fifty-five indicated that single women are far more prone than married women to physical illness. Singles suffer more chronic conditions and spend more days in bed than those with wedding rings. However, the likelihood of a divorced woman dying from cancer, for example, is much lower than for a divorced man, whose risk is two to four times greater. A divorced woman's odds of dying in a given year from cancer of the mouth, digestive organs, lungs, or breast are 13 percent to 67 percent higher than those of a married woman of the same age.[15]

Linda Waite and Mary Elizabeth Hughes found that wives nearing retirement age were about 30 percent more likely to rate their health excellent or very good than were same-aged single women, and almost 40 percent less likely to say their health is only fair or poor.[16] (We note in chapter 3 that cohabiting women are three times as likely to suffer from depression and are more likely to have other health disorders than married couples.)

Married Couples Live Longer

"Being unmarried can actually be a greater risk to one's life than having heart disease or cancer," Waite and Gallagher assert. "For example, having heart disease shortens the average man's life span by slightly less than six years. But being unmarried chops almost *ten years* off a man's life. Similarly, not being married will shorten a woman's life span by more years than would being married and having cancer or living in poverty."[17]

Statisticians Bernard Cohen and I-Sing Lee make a stark conclusion: "Being unmarried is one of the greatest risks that people voluntarily subject themselves to."[18]

Using data from a large national study begun in 1968, Lee Lillard and Linda Waite found that almost nine out of ten married men (88 percent) alive at age forty-eight would still be alive at age sixty-five. By contrast, just six out of ten (63 percent) never-married men would be alive at age sixty-five. A divorced man has only a 65 percent chance of survival to age sixty-five; 69 percent of widowed men will be alive by age sixty-five. For women, the relationship of marriage to life span is similar but less striking. A married woman aged forty-eight has a 92 percent chance of living to sixty-five, but a divorced woman's odds drop to 82 percent.[19]

How do these statistics relate to cohabitation? Waite and Gallagher explain:

> Unlike getting married, merely moving in together did not seem to motivate young men and women to reduce unhealthy behavior. During their twenties, young men and women who live together showed very high and increasing rates of health-destroying and dangerous behaviors. Those who married, by contrast, started out with moderate levels of smoking, drinking, and drug use during high school but improved on all fronts, often dramatically. . . .
>
> The evidence from four decades of research is surprisingly clear: a good marriage is both men's and women's best bet for living a long and healthy life.[20]

"Loneliness is a lethal force with the power to break the human heart," writes James J. Lynch in *A Cry Unheard*.[21] A married couple cares for each other. For example, a wife watches their diet and objects if her husband pours a second drink. But when one of them dies or they divorce, the will to live is extinguished for many. As a consequence, many abandoned partners suffer depression—and depressed people are four times more likely to develop heart disease than those who are not depressed and are four times more likely to die within six months. Divorced men are three times as likely to commit suicide as married men. The risk of suicide for divorced women is double that of married women.

Married Couples Are Wealthier

A 2002 study by Janet Wilmoth and Gregor Koso found that those who never marry experience a 75 percent reduction in wealth compared to those continuously married. The study also reports a 73 percent wealth reduction among those who divorced and did not remarry.

"Married men earn between 10 and 40 percent more than do single men with similar education and job histories," according to the report "Why Marriage Matters." Why? "Married men appear to have a greater work commitment, lower quit rates, and healthier and more stable personal routines (including sleep, diet, and alcohol consumption). Husbands also benefit from both the work effort and emotional support that they receive from their wives."[22]

Not surprisingly, married couples also accumulate more assets than the divorced or never married. What is surprising, however, is that as singles approach retirement age, the never-married have about the same assets as the divorced and have saved only about a third of what married couples have accumulated. The actual numbers are startling: according to *The Case for Marriage,* "On the verge of retirement, the typical married couple had accumulated about $410,000 (or $205,000 each), compared to about $167,000 for the never-married, just under $154,000 for the divorced, about $151,000 for the widowed, and just under $96,000 for the separated."[23]

Curiously, the married couple lavished thousands of dollars on their kids' clothes, music lessons, summer camp, braces, and college tuition, while the never-married had no such drains on their bank accounts.

Marrying offers balance. Spouses are invested in each other and in the well-being of their joint future. He proposes to buy a new car; she says, "That's a waste of our money. Let's remodel the screen porch and turn it into a sunroom." Result: the investment increases the value of their home. The single guy buys the car or vacations in Cancun and by retirement can claim fewer assets.

What is the relevance of this for cohabitors? The unmarried will lead shorter lives and have fewer assets than married couples. "Strikingly, for cohabitors (unlike spouses), the length of the relationship has no effect on wealth accumulation. Something about being married causes people to save and acquire more."[24]

Additional evidence that married couples are wealthier than cohabiting couples comes from the U.S. Census, which reported that in 2005 the average income for a married-couple household with a related child under age eighteen was $89,234. That compares with only $54,792 for an unmarried-couple household with a child.[25] In other words, a married couple earns 61.4 percent more than a cohabiting couple. A single female householder with a child earned only $36,330, and a male head of household $54,929. Clearly, marriage brings substantial economic dividends that are unavailable with the counterfeit of marriage called cohabitation. By dismissing marriage, cohabiting couples are condemning themselves to a much lower standard of living.

Married People Have More and Better Sex Than Singles

Sex and the City, Friends, and other sitcoms imply that the happiest people are those who jump in bed with someone new every Friday night or those who are cohabiting. The clear impression is that single people have more sex and better sex than married couples. But this is far from the truth. Actually, singles have less frequent and less satisfactory sex than married couples do.

Waite and Gallagher report: "According to the National Sex Survey, 43 percent of the married men reported that they had sex at least twice a week. Only 26 percent of the single men (not cohabiting) said they had sex this often. . . . The picture is much the same for women: Wives had more active sex lives than all types of single women except cohabitors: 39 percent of married women had sex two or three times a week or more, compared to 20 percent of single women."[26]

Citing the National Sex Survey of nearly 3,500 American adults in 1992 and another study by Scott Stanley and Howard Markman, co-directors of the Center for Marital and Family Studies at the University of Denver, Waite and Gallagher summarize: "Married people have both more and more satisfying sex than singles do. They not only have sex more often, but they enjoy it more, both physically and emotionally, than do their unmarried counterparts."[27]

Specifically, "42 percent of married women interviewed in the National Sex Survey said they found sex extremely emotionally and physically satisfying, compared to just 31 percent of single women who had a sex partner."[28] In fact, the authors report:

> Married women are almost twice as likely as divorced and never-married women to have a sex life that (a) exists and (b) is extremely emotionally satisfying. About four out of ten wives have a sexual partner who leaves them extremely emotionally satisfied, compared to only about one out of four never-married women and one out of five previously married women.
>
> What about cohabitors? While cohabiting couples have at least as much sex as the married, they don't seem to enjoy it quite as much. For men, having a wife beats shacking up by a wide margin: 48 percent of husbands say sex with their partner is extremely satisfying emotionally, compared to just 37 percent of cohabiting men.[29]

Why is married sex more satisfying? "The secret ingredient that marriage adds is commitment. For women, the idea that committed sex is better sex is almost a truism. . . . Women, not men, get pregnant. Therefore, women have a stronger incentive than men to make sure their sexual partners care for them and are likely to care for their children."[30]

Stanley reported that married couples and cohabitors have a similar frequency of sex, if adjusted for the length of the relationship, but married couples were more satisfied with sex. That's "partly a function of the overall sense of security and commitment that tends to be greater in marriage than cohabitation."[31]

How ironic that one of the compelling reasons for couples to cohabit is the availability of sex. Yet, ultimately, by sidestepping marriage—the right and best way to live together—the couple ends up with "sex lite."

The bottom line is simple. "Marriage for most people is the means to health, happiness, wealth, sex, and long life," write Waite and Gallagher. "In love, victory goes not to the half-hearted but to the brave: to those ordinary people who dare to take on the extraordinary commitment marriage represents."[32]

CHAPTER 6

The Church's Responsibility

If the watchman sees the enemy coming and doesn't sound the alarm to warn the people, he is responsible for their captivity.

Ezekiel 33:6 *NLT*

When so many young people have never seen a good marriage, we have a moral obligation to try to intervene preventively.

Judith Wallerstein, Julia M. Lewis, Sandra Blakeslee,
The Unexpected Legacy of Divorce

IN WRITING TO the Corinthians, Paul advised: "Flee from sexual immorality. All other sins a man commits are outside his body, but he who sins sexually sins against his own body. Do you not know that your body is a temple of the Holy Spirit, who is in you, whom you have received from God? You are not your own; you were bought at a price. Therefore honor God with your body" (1 Corinthians 6:18–20). The King James Version translates the first verse of that scripture more starkly: "Flee fornication."

What is cohabitation but fornication raised to the *n*th power? The church is the one institution society expects to take a stand on this issue. Yet few do. W. Bradford Wilcox of the University of Virginia writes that America's houses of worship are "traditionally the most important custodians of marriage in the nation," yet they "have been unable and unwilling to foster the beliefs and virtues that make for a strong marriage culture."

The American church has abdicated its responsibility to make the case for chastity, so it's not surprising that it hasn't addressed cohabitation. Most churches simply ignore the issue, rationalizing, "We're helping cohabiting couples legitimize their relationships if we marry them." However, if, for example, Hector and Teresa had married without the rigorous marriage preparation that we gave them (detailed in chapter 9), they would have divorced. Cohabitation often corrupts relationships between unmarried men and women. That corruption carries over into the marriage.

Because of the church's lack of leadership and clear stand on this issue, even Christians are unwittingly drawn into the danger-fraught lifestyle of cohabitation.

The Barna Group reported:

- 25 percent of those living together are "born-again" Christians;
- 37 percent say they are Christians;
- 42 percent of cohabitors have a non-Christian faith;
- 45 percent of those living together are not religious; and
- 51 percent of cohabitors identify themselves as atheists.[1]

What's significant about these poll results is how cohabiting couples contrast with the general American population: two-thirds are church members, and two fifths attend church in any given week.[2]

A 2004 Barna poll explored another related area in which the church is failing couples. In many Christian congregations, the divorce rate is even higher than that of nonbelievers: 39 percent of Protestants had divorced, compared to only 37 percent of atheists/agnostics. Only Catholics have significantly lower divorce rates, of 25 percent.

Why such a dramatic statistical difference between Protestants and Catholics? Perhaps the answer is that Catholic marriage preparation tends to be far more rigorous than that provided by most Protestant churches. The Catholic Church requires couples asking to be married to set a wedding date six to twelve months from their first meeting with the priest. By contrast, Protestants have no time requirement. Additionally, a high percentage of Catholic churches require couples to take a premarital inventory and discuss the relational issues it reveals with a priest, a married deacon and his wife, or a sponsor couple (a Mentor Couple).

On the positive side, a growing number of Protestant churches require couples to take such an inventory; however, *two-thirds* of engaged couples in America are not given that opportunity.

Certainly another factor in the lower Catholic divorce rate is the church's firm stand against divorce, which it asserts is always wrong.[3] This attitude and the requirement of thorough marriage preparation indicate that Catholics take marriage much more seriously than Protestants do. And that makes a difference. The Catholic divorce rate is 56 percent lower than that of Protestants.

Still, neither Catholic nor Protestant churches seem to be doing an adequate job when it comes to the cohabitation issue. If a couple is living together, the church (Catholic or Protestant)—the one institution society expects to voice expectations of chastity before marriage—is oddly silent. Curiously, pastors rarely preach against cohabitation or teach about its dangers. I've asked thousands of clergy in scores of cities if they've ever spoken on the issue from the pulpit. One in fifty raises a hand. Nor do they know what to say when cohabiting couples ask to be married in their churches.

Ministers typically avoid the issue by saying nothing. Parents are flummoxed about how to react to their own cohabiting children, given the silence of their moral leaders.

What explains the church's abject capitulation on this moral issue?

Clergy know that cohabitation is unbiblical. They may not know that a cohabiting couple is more likely to divorce if they marry. Either way, they fear that raising the issue will prompt the couple to go elsewhere to marry. Protestant pastors are competing with one another for new members and are loathe to make demands that might lose new prospects.[4] The fastest growing churches in America call themselves "seeker friendly." That often means, with regard to marriage preparation, that few demands are made other than attending two to four "premarital counseling sessions," some of which may involve only watching videos or planning the wedding ceremony. Mainline churches are likely to require fewer premarital sessions than evangelicals, and the requirement of an inventory is spotty. Rarely do churches have Marriage Mentors.

Religion's Impact on Marriage

In families with children, couples who are married are 51 percent more likely to attend religious services weekly than unmarried cohabiting couples. A study of the National Survey of America's Families, a research group, reports that 40 percent of married parents attended church weekly, compared to only 26.4 percent of unwed parents.

Churches of all denominations wink at cohabitation. Why? Because cohabitation is so endemic in our culture that many pastors have come to regard cohabiting couples as the norm. They evidence no higher morality standards than those seen on the TV sitcom *Friends*. Such was the stance of Teresa and Hector's pastor. When the couple asked him if it was all right to live together, he responded, "It is not living together that's the problem; it's extramarital sex. It's okay as long as you're engaged to be married." He didn't advise them to stop having premarital sex or to live apart until they were married.

In fairness to ministers, however, most simply don't know how to address the sensitive issue of cohabitation. They know it's wrong, but in their desire to make things right, they rush to erase the problem (or "fix" the sin) by either ignoring it or pretending not to notice that the couple shares the same address. Cohabitation is an issue that has surfaced so recently that it's not even covered in most seminary curricula.

The church, which marries 86 percent of couples according to a Peter Hart poll, has a moral responsibility to provide couples considering marriage a better way to test their relationship.[5] This is a task that organized religion should address. Yet the roles of promoter and protector of marriage have been badly neglected by most churches.

COHABITATION: A SENSITIVE ISSUE FOR PASTORS

Many pastors treat the subject of living together as a "third rail" to be avoided because they are ill-equipped to handle it. Typically, clergy adopt one of the following stances toward cohabiting couples who seek to be married in the church:

1. Ignore the Couple's Living Arrangements

Often pastors pretend they don't know the couple is cohabiting. The couple joins in this charade by pretending that they don't know the pastor knows. Clergy lower the standards of the church to accommodate the couple instead of raising them to higher, scriptural principles.

All parties lose in this conspiracy of silence: the couple, the pastor, the church, and society.

Every town has "Marrying Sams" who will marry anyone for a fee. Many pastors fear that if they ask the couple to move apart, they will simply go across town to a less-demanding church. A Protestant pastor in a typical church of one hundred to two hundred people would like to have this couple become members of his congregation. Consequently, some pastors brush aside their feelings or convictions on the matter and pretend they don't notice the couple has the same address. They rationalize, "At least they're making the relationship right by getting married," and hope for the best.

"Most pastors face this scenario repeatedly," Rev. Jeff Meyers of Christ Lutheran Church, Overland Park, Kansas, confessed. " 'What can I do?' many of us ask. 'Do I encourage them to marry quickly to make it 'right'? *Honestly, since when does a wedding solve a sin problem?*"

Perhaps a pastor is unaware of the high risk of divorce for cohabiting couples. Or he or she may rationalize, "If I marry them, maybe they'll join the church, and I can help them grow in their faith and become more moral." However, all live-in relationships are at risk, and the pastor is the natural "point person" to address this problem. Such a "Don't ask, don't tell" policy is in neither the couple's nor the church's best interest.

The problem of couples living together before marriage has mushroomed to such gargantuan proportions that the church can no longer ignore it. Pastoral ignorance of the consequences of living together is not an excuse for failing to address the devastating impact it has on couples, their relationships, their ensuing marriage, and their children.

2. Turn the Couple Away

This is one way to avoid theological conflict. However, it's important to realize that by refusing to marry cohabiting couples, clergy may be inadvertently sending the message that the couple is unworthy and unwelcome. The couple will learn two things:

1. The church that has marriage standards is judgmental and hostile.
2. Stepping over the threshold of a church is uninviting and intimidating.

Such a forbidding stance by the pastor might well be remembered by the couple as such an unpleasant event that it could deter them from future religious activity altogether.

3. Demand That the Couple Move Apart Before the Wedding

While well intentioned, this demand by itself might send a message that submitting to it will, in itself, ensure success in marriage. The truth is that some cohabiting couples don't have a strong enough relationship to marry and shouldn't marry. However, they won't understand this unless they go through a rigorous marriage preparation process. True, moving apart is a step in the right direction toward building a healthy union. It will end some arguments. However, it cannot undo the damage that has already been done to the relationship. Couples need to address the risk factors they have incurred by living together and to replace dysfunctional patterns with healthy behaviors.

Another problem with demanding that couples move apart is that many will simply choose a less-demanding church, which is in no one's interest.

4. Suggest the Couple Have a Civil Wedding First

Some pastors tell the couple, "First, have a civil wedding at the courthouse to legalize your relationship." Or, "I'll perform a quiet service here in my church office if you promise to go through our marriage preparation process. Then you can have a church wedding later." The danger here is that in their haste to legalize the couple's living arrangements, clergy may be rushing couples into marriage who shouldn't marry at all. If this is the case, ministers may inadvertently be rushing couples toward divorce as well.

Nearly a fifth of couples who participate in rigorous marriage preparation decide *not* to marry. What if they come to the conclusion that they shouldn't be married three months after their rushed civil or church-office wedding? Sadly, the pastor will have participated in further perpetuating unresolved relationship issues in his haste to make the couple acceptable in the eyes of the church.

HOPE: A PROVEN WAY TO HELP COHABITING COUPLES

The goal of this book is to offer hope and direction for cohabiting couples and the churches that serve them. There is an alternative to cohabitation, and it is a proven path of success. Unfortunately, this road to marital success has been largely unavailable to couples. Why?

- Two-thirds of churches do not require a premarital inventory of couples they marry.
- In the eight hundred thousand congregations that do offer an inventory, pastors meet with the couple for no more than an hour to discuss the questionnaire's results. Typically, these pastors address just three areas of strength and three areas where growth is needed. The couple's responses on the remaining 150 issues are ignored.
- Few churches have recruited and trained Mentor Couples who are willing and able to prepare couples for marriage.

Marriage Savers, the organization Harriet and I founded, trains volunteer lay couples to be Mentor Couples who review *every* issue covered by an inventory, devoting fifteen to eighteen hours to serious, helpful discussion over the course of five or six sessions. These mentors also administer a series of exercises that will help couples improve their ability to resolve conflict, explore each other's family history and its potential impact on their relationship, prepare a budget, and set personal and joint goals.

In addition, Mentor Couples provide a model of successful marriage—imperfect, but healthy. Every congregation has couples who could be equipped to assist and support other couples not only to prepare for a lifelong marriage but also to enrich existing marriages and restore those that are troubled. Tragically, the wisdom of Mentor Couples remains untapped in most churches because clergy have not recognized their value.

Because so few churches offer a workable, effective strategy to help couples achieve a successful marriage, America's congregations bear substantial responsibility for our high divorce rate.

The good news is that because churches are intimately involved in the majority of weddings and in counseling couples in marital distress, they are perfectly poised to step into the gap to help make marriages work. Instead of being part of the problem, churches can be part of the answer.

We recommend a new way for pastors to deal with cohabiting couples.

WELCOME ALL COUPLES TO MARRIAGE PREP—MARRY ONLY THOSE LIVING APART

Tell the couple, "Yes, I would like to perform your wedding. However, because you're living together, which is not in your—or the church's—

best interest, I urge you to move apart until the wedding. This church will not marry any cohabiting couples who have not moved apart. However, whether you move apart or not, we want to give you thorough marriage preparation. We will offer you the same marriage preparation we offer couples who marry here."

Our experience at our own church and in our national ministry, Marriage Savers, is that most couples who are treated with honesty and concern ultimately do move apart, or at least into separate bedrooms.

Adopting this strategy is positive and welcoming to the cohabiting couple, instead of being intimidating and judgmental. Also, the church can maintain a biblical standard by not marrying cohabiting couples while still demonstrating concern for them by offering rigorous marriage preparation regardless of whether they move apart.

The result of this strategy in the church Harriet and I attend has been a divorce rate of less than 5 percent over a decade.

This approach stands against the sin while loving the sinner. While few cohabiting couples are religiously active, many desire a church wedding. Consequently, the church has great access and a superb opportunity to positively impact cohabiting couples wanting to marry.

When churches handle the challenge of cohabitation correctly, offering guidance and support to form healthy, lifelong unions, everybody wins—the couple, their children, the church, and the culture!

Springfield, Ohio, is a community example with hard data. From January 1, 2004, through December 9, 2004, 865 marriage licenses were issued to couples in Clark County, a conservative, semirural county of 146,000 people. Springfield is its largest city. Of those who married, 58 percent of couples shared the same address before their wedding. More than half (52 percent) were remarriages for at least one partner. One might presume that most of these cohabiting couples were not religious. Indeed, those married by judges or mayors in civil ceremonies were cohabiting in 79 percent of the cases, and 65 percent of those marriages involved a partner who had been previously married. However, 80 percent of the weddings were performed by clergy. Of the couples who had church weddings, 46 percent were cohabiting and 49 percent involved remarriages. By not asking these couples to live separately, the clergy were unwittingly but certainly condemning many of them to divorce.

Strong language. But here's evidence: from 1999 to 2003, the average divorce rate in Clark County was an alarming 97 percent, or double the U.S. average of 47.5 percent during those years.

The American church is asleep on this issue, but it can awake and embrace the strategies that some congregations have adopted to reverse these trends. *Divorce rates can be reduced to near zero in a church, and cut 15 to 50 percent across a metropolitan area.*

Think that's an unrealistic claim? Consider the evidence. In September 2004, Harriet and I helped the clergy of Springfield, Ohio, create a Community Marriage Policy (CMP). In this covenant, the clergy pledged to require couples they married to take four to six months of marriage preparation with a Mentor Couple. More than 125 pastors—the vast majority of clergy in Springfield—have agreed to these premarital standards and to other strategies to enrich existing marriages, restore troubled ones, reconcile separated couples, and help stepfamilies be successful.

The result? Within two years, by the end of 2006, Springfield's divorce rate fell from an average of 857 dissolutions a year to 711. That is a significant drop of 17 percent.

Nor is this unusual. By August 2007, the clergy of 220 cities had adopted a Community Marriage Policy like that of Springfield. Some cities have slashed divorce rates by 50 percent or more, such as Austin, Texas, and the Kansas City, Kansas, metropolitan area.

Cohabitation rates can be reduced as well. The second half of this book outlines how any congregation or community can implement proven steps for doing this, and suggests a healthier and more appropriate way for cohabiting couples to test their relationships.

Most churches today are *wedding factories*. The majority of engaged couples are taught little or nothing by the church about how to make a marriage work. This failure is particularly distressing because marriage is a pivotal point in a couple's life. Since the majority of weddings are performed by clergy, the church has extraordinary and strategic access to exert positive influence.

Tragically, it is currently squandering that unique opportunity. Ask pastors if they require premarital counseling for engaged couples, and most will respond, "Yes, I require *X* number of counseling sessions." However, research suggests that America's churches generally do a poor job of marriage preparation. In 1999 the Family Research Council commissioned a poll by Wirthlin Worldwide of married couples asking if they'd had premarital counseling: 73 percent said no. Another 12 percent said they met with a pastor once or twice. Only 15 percent of couples remembered meaningful premarital counseling.

These numbers were substantiated in a 2004 survey of ninety pastors in Springfield, Ohio, by the Marriage Resource Center. It revealed that only 30 percent of churches offered any formal marriage preparation, and only half of those required a premarital inventory or more than two counseling sessions (thus the aforementioned 15 percent).

The impact of wedding-factory churches on marriage in America has been disastrous.

Yet as the Springfield example demonstrates, there is hope when churches embrace their responsibility to help couples in a more effective way.

A BETTER ANSWER FOR CHURCHES AND COUPLES

A better answer involves five key actions:

1. Require a Premarital Inventory

A premarital inventory gives couples an objective assessment of their relational strengths and those areas in which they need to grow. "It offers couples an opportunity to talk about things they didn't even know they needed to talk about," according to Dr. Barbara Markey, primary author of the FOCCUS premarital inventory. It also serves as a bridge between the premarital couple and a mature, trained Mentor Couple in a healthy marriage. Only a third of churches today require such an inventory.

2. Train a Core of Mentor Couples

Willing couples in solid marriages can be found in any congregation and equipped to help cohabiting couples choose a better path. Trained Marriage Mentors can help improve the quality of the mentored couple's relationship by facilitating discussion of relationship issues brought to light by the premarital inventory. Mentors can also make a compelling case for the couple to move apart and remain chaste until the wedding. Currently, less than 5 percent of churches have Mentor Couples.

3. Teach Skills to Resolve Conflict

Mentors can model and administer a series of relationship exercises, most of which are designed to improve the engaged couple's life skills of healthy communication and conflict resolution. Among couples participating in our church's premarital program with mentors who offer an inventory, interpret it, and teach problem-solving skills over three to four months, *the divorce rate was only 3 percent over a decade.*[6]

4. Establish Church Policy for Cohabiting Couples

To deal effectively with the growing issue of cohabiting couples wishing to marry, churches need to have a written policy that their governing board has approved. Then, when a cohabiting couple asks to be married, the pastor can refer to the church's official marriage policy. The policy should be welcoming, offering an array of proven and effective marital preparation steps, while outlining the church's biblically based standards. A typical marriage policy would include the following statements:

- All engaged couples—whether they are living together or not—are invited to participate in the church's premarital program. All couples planning to be married in the church are required to complete the program. This includes remarrying couples who have experienced a divorce or who are widowed.
- No cohabiting couple will be married by the church if they do not live separately for a minimum number of months before the wedding. However, if such a couple abides by these guidelines, they can be married in the church.
- If a cohabiting couple refuses to move apart, they should still be offered the opportunity to take an inventory with a Mentor Couple and be trained in communication and conflict-resolution skills, etc. The hope is that mentors will persuade them to move apart during the mentoring.

- The pastor will have broad discretion regarding marrying cohabiting couples if, for example, the woman is pregnant. In such a case, the couple would still be expected to complete the premarital process after the wedding.
- Seriously dating couples should be included in the church's premarital program. Such a step will deter couples from moving in together as well as help them think through their choice of a potential life mate *before* a wedding announcement, avoiding future pain and embarrassment.

5. Educate the Cohabiting Couple

During the initial meeting, the pastor should inform the cohabiting couple about the risks of living together, providing answers to common myths. He should encourage the couple to move apart.

For more than a decade Rev. Jeff has taken this position with cohabiting couples. "I tell them the truth—that cohabitation is not biblical and that it does not work. The couples are very responsive. At least 80 percent separate. I won't marry the others, which sometimes comes as a shock to the parents."

This is a strategy many pastors call "standing against the sin while loving the sinner."

Some couples will refuse to live separately or to abstain from sex. Harriet and I mentored Jack and Jan, who had drifted into cohabitation when one of their leases was about to expire. They had decided to marry and wanted to save money. When I asked if they would consider moving apart, Jan replied, "No, I don't want to. I'm used to him now. I like having him around." We mentored them nevertheless but became increasingly aware, after four sessions, that they were completing none of their homework assignments. Their relationship, as a result, did not grow. I spoke with them about this, saying, "We willingly donate our time at no cost to help you. Yet you do so little to help yourselves." They did not return.

Mentor Couples will be able to persuade some couples to move apart or to move into separate bedrooms and discontinue sex until the wedding. But the success rate is much higher if a pastor takes a stand. Ideally, the Mentor Couple's job is to help couples build successful relationships after the pastor has persuaded them to live separately.

Of fifty-six couples Harriet and I have mentored personally since 1991, most of whom were not cohabiting, nine decided on their own not to marry. Of those who did marry, none whom we know of have divorced. Our church's divorce rate is similar—only 7 couples divorced or separated over a decade, out of 288 couples.

BEYOND PREMARITAL PREPARATION: DIVORCE-PROOFING YOUR CHURCH

Premarital marriage preparation, although key to launching healthy unions, should be viewed as only one aspect of a church's marriage ministry. Marriages need support at *every* stage to be successful, especially the marriages of couples who had previously lived together. Like all couples, they need marriage enrichment; but many also will need help restoring a troubled marriage or learning how to make a stepfamily successful.

All marriages are at risk of divorce. Therefore, it's imperative for churches to place a "safety net" under *every* couple's marriage by adopting a holistic approach to protect marriages. Churches that prepare couples for a healthy, lifelong marriage need to be equally concerned about enriching existing marriages, restoring couples in crisis, reconciling the separated, and helping stepfamilies to be successful. Most

High Divorce and Cohabitation Rates Plague the Church

- America, the most religious modern nation, is the world's most divorcing country.[7] Gallup polls estimate that two thirds of Americans are members of a church or synagogue, and two fifths attend services in any given week.[8] These attendance figures are four times those of France or Germany, yet those countries' divorce rates are half that of the United States.[9] Organized religion in America has access to most marrying couples, yet half of new marriages end in divorce. It seems obvious that churches and synagogues are doing something wrong.

- A September 8, 2004, George Barna poll estimated that three out of four adults (73 percent) have been married, but only half (51 percent) are currently married, not including 3 percent who are currently separated from their spouses. Among those who have married, 35 percent have also divorced. One out of five adults (18 percent) who has ever divorced has divorced multiple times.[10]

- Atheists and agnostics are less likely to have divorced than Protestants. Barna wrote, "You can understand why atheists and agnostics might have a high rate of divorce since they are less likely to believe in such concepts as sin, absolute moral truth and judgment." Yet only 37 percent of those nonbelievers have divorced, compared to 39 percent of all Protestants. Of more deeply committed born-

(continued)

again Americans, 35 percent have divorced—virtually the same percentage as atheists and agnostics.

- Twenty-three percent of born-again Christians have divorced two or more times.
- Among the largest Protestant groups, 44 percent of Pentecostals have divorced, while Presbyterian had the fewest divorces, at 28 percent.

Religious Background	Percentage Ever Divorced
Catholic	25
Presbyterian	28
Born-again Christian	35
Atheist/Agnostic	37
All Protestant	39
Pentecostal	44

Barna analyzed the data according to the ages at which survey respondents were divorced and the age at which those who were born-again Christians accepted Jesus Christ as their savior. "The data suggest that relatively few divorced Christians experienced their divorce before accepting Christ as their savior," he explained. "If we eliminate those who became Christian after their divorce, the divorce figure among born-again adults drops to 34 percent—statistically identical to the figure among non-Christians" (35 percent).

churches deal only with premarital or troubled couples. Working with engaged couples is fun. It's a happy time. Struggling couples are the "squeaky wheels" whose problems can't wait, so they get attention.

But what about the majority of couples in average or ho-hum marriages? See chapter 10 for more details on a comprehensive marriage strategy.

Couples in stable marriages typically receive little or no attention—yet they are the financial backbone and the volunteer service core of the church. Engaged couples and newlyweds often are not in a position to be generous in their giving, and troubled couples, who may be considering divorce, are distracted or may be in financial distress. Homeowners give their automobiles and lawnmowers an annual tune-up, yet the church—the overseer of God's first institution, marriage—fails dismally to provide an "annual checkup" for the relationships of married couples. All marriages grow flat over time and need to be revitalized. Yet even those who especially need help—millions of couples who once cohabited and are therefore at risk and struggling to make their marriages work—rarely receive support.

Every pastor should seek ways to "divorce-proof" the church. A million couples divorce each year. Their marital failure impacts another million children annually, who will be scarred by their parents' divorce. For example, adult children of divorce are more likely to cohabit and divorce than children raised in intact families.

Every church has couples who are separated. However, separation typically is regarded as a prelude to divorce rather than an opportunity for couples to reflect, reassess, and recommit to the marriage. Ideally, it should be a time dedicated to self-evaluation and personal growth. (See chapter 10 for information on "Reconciling God's Way," a program to help separated couples.) Growth spawns positive change, which often attracts back a disgruntled mate.

Nearly half of all marriages involve couples who have experienced one or more failed marriages. These remarriages are more likely to fail than first marriages. Studies show that 60 percent of second marriages end in divorce, 70 percent if the individuals have children from a previous marriage or relationship or are entering a third marriage. Yet scant support is given to remarriages in the church. (See chapter 10 for information on creating a Stepfamily Support Group.)

If churches are serious about caring for the future well-being of their congregations, they need to provide ministries that support marriage.

GOOD NEWS OF PROFOUND IMPORTANCE

As the writer of a nationally syndicated newspaper column, "Ethics & Religion," since 1981, I have had the privilege of researching and reporting about many innovations to strengthen marriages. Often the best initiatives were pioneered by a single church. Harriet and I created the premarital strategy described in this book at our own church. Other churches designed answers for marriage restoration, reconciliation, and successful stepfamilies, the details of which are explored in the last chapter of this book. For example:

- A United Methodist Church in Roswell, Georgia, developed a Stepfamily Support Group to help couples with children from a previous marriage or relationship to be successful. Instead of *losing* 70 percent of stepfamilies to divorce, Stepfamily Support Groups help *save* 80 percent of such marriages.[11]
- St. David's Episcopal Church in Jacksonville, Florida, pioneered a Marriage Ministry to train couples whose marriages had once nearly failed to mentor those in current crisis. Out of forty troubled marriages, thirty-eight were saved.
- Joe and Michelle Williams created the highly effective course "Reconciling God's Way" at their evangelical church in Modesto, California. It helps 50 to 75 percent of separated couples to reconcile.

Such success stories are good news—and that good news is profoundly important. David Popenoe and Barbara Dafoe Whitehead eloquently summarized what is at stake regarding marriage in *The State of Our Unions: 2002*: "Marriage is a fundamental social institution. It is central to the nurture and raising of children. It is the 'social glue' that reliably attaches fathers to children. It contributes to the physical, emotional and economic health of men, women and children, and thus to the nation as a whole. It is also one of the most highly prized of all human relationships and a central life goal of most Americans."[12]

The stakes are high. The future well-being of our children and our children's children is at risk. The evidence is clear. We now know unequivocally that cohabitation doesn't work. Churches—the gatekeepers of weddings—can delay no longer. They must educate, equip, and elevate marriage to the position of honor it deserves.

Organized religion has unwittingly contributed to America's high divorce and soaring cohabitation rates. But it can become the architect of a new culture that honors marriage once again.

CHAPTER 7

The Right Way to Test a Relationship

Test everything. Hold on to the good. Avoid every kind of evil.

1 Thessalonians 5:21–22

The inventory was an eye opener—surprisingly helpful. It prompted discussion and opened communication on issues that, alone, we either rarely touched on or had not discussed well, so that strengths and weaknesses were revealed.

George, a mentoree

MARRIAGE INSURANCE

When Harriet and I begin mentoring a cohabiting couple, this is our approach. We ask the couple "How would you like marriage insurance—a 95 percent guarantee that if you marry, you'll 'live happily ever after'?" That's the mirror opposite of the 80 plus percent chance of failure you'll be risking if you continue living together.

How can you get marriage insurance? First, move apart. That's the only sure way you can obtain the perspective needed to see your relationship objectively. This is the most important step you can take to increase your odds of a lifelong marriage.[1]

Second, you need rigorous marriage preparation that involves meeting with us as your trained Mentor Couple for about four months. We can help your relationship grow and help you address differences.

We do that by administering a premarital inventory. This is a much better way to test the relationship than by living together. In addition, we will teach you practical communication and conflict resolution skills. You will find this useful because poor problem solving is the most common reason couples divorce.

Incidentally, one couple in five who is mentored decides not to marry. Of the fifty-six couples we have mentored personally, nine decided not to marry. Let me emphasize that we did not advise them to break up; that was a decision they reached on their own.

Research indicates that couples who break an engagement after taking an inventory have the same scores as those who marry and later divorce. Those broken engagements are avoided divorces. Better the broken engagement than a broken marriage with two kids.

However, to our knowledge, none of the forty-seven couples we mentored who married have divorced. The failure rate in our church with 288 couples over a decade is only 3 percent.

That's a 97 percent success rate. *That's "marriage insurance."*

"Interested?" we ask couples. Most say yes . . . but they don't want to move apart, let alone abstain from sex.

Let's take a look at the two components essential for this type of "marriage insurance": (1) moving apart, and (2) rigorous marriage preparation.

If You're Living Together, Move Apart

The best single step cohabiting couples can take to increase their odds of a lifelong marriage is to move apart. No couple who is living together wants to hear such advice. We also urge every couple—whether living together or not—to consider signing an "Optional Premarital Sexual Covenant," in which they pledge to defer sex until the wedding.[2] This is equally unwelcome advice.

However, our role as representatives of the church is not to coddle cohabiting couples but to encourage them to strive to do what they need to do to succeed in marriage—not merely what they want to do. Those who cohabit are unwittingly playing with fire, inviting risks into their relationship. They deserve guidance on how they can achieve lasting and happy marriages.

Cohabiting couples are likely to defend their living arrangements by citing commonly believed myths about living together. We suggest respectfully rebutting these myths with facts (see pages 5–6 for quick answers to a dozen widely believed myths).[3] We assure couples that the inconvenience of moving apart now is far less than the pain of a possible divorce later. If partners truly love each other and think the relationship is worthwhile, they can set aside short-term gratification for long-term benefits.

In our *Marriage Savers Mentors' Guide* we outline five benefits cohabiting couples will glean by agreeing to move apart.[4] We suggest that these benefits be reviewed with couples who are living together:

1. Moving Apart Offers a New Beginning

Living independently provides couples with an opportunity to see marriage as a decisive new beginning—a watershed moment in their lives. It's a chance for them to take a "fresh look" at each other. Living apart will be a radically different experience from living together and will help the cohabiting couple deal with problems that arose in the relationship before full marital commitment was made.

2. Moving Apart Solves Some Problems

Arguments over money, particularly over what is a fair share for each to contribute toward rent, utilities, and groceries, will cease. This is a path to new self-respect as well as respect for one's future spouse. By living separately, the relationship is put on a healthier and more biblical footing.

3. MOVING APART ALIGNS THE RELATIONSHIP WITH GOD'S WILL

Scripture calls couples to chastity before marriage and fidelity within marriage. If couples expect God to bless their relationship, they need to consider following his guidelines.

Biblical standards call us to God's best. The blessings for each partner and for the relationship will be abundant if cohabiting couples choose to begin abiding by God's ways by moving apart and remaining chaste from this point until the wedding. Couples have an opportunity to practice chastity while they are single so that when they do marry, they will have demonstrated to their spouse that they can be faithful. Fidelity builds trust. We base our trust on our future spouse's past behavior.

4. MOVING APART OFFERS TIME AND SPACE TO EXAMINE ATTITUDES AND PATTERNS

It's difficult for a premarital couple to learn and practice communication and problem-solving skills when they're sexually bonded. When they're in conflict, they often turn to sex to restore emotional intimacy. This pattern leaves relational issues unresolved. The closeness that comes with physical intimacy is shallow and temporary, evaporating when the next argument erupts over the same issue. Root problems remain unaddressed, and the couple grows increasingly frustrated with their pattern of high conflict and unresolved issues.

If, however, the couple sets aside sex and develops healthy communication skills, they will grow closer through their efforts to understand one another and reach consensus.

5. MOVING APART OFFERS HOPE

Cohabiting couples who move apart and enroll in a rigorous preparation process fare better in marriage than similar couples who do not—a hopeful truth mentors should convey.

The couples coming to you have already decided to marry, which is positive. They are to be commended for their good intentions. Mentors can be a source of encouragement, helping a couple build upon their decision to marry and take a premarital counseling course.

Even though they made a previous decision to live together, and some damage has been done to their relationship, mentors must avoid planting the seeds of a self-fulfilling prophesy of marital failure. A punitive tone is unhelpful and will only alienate them. Mentor Couples should not perceive themselves as scolding parents, moralizing theologians, or statistical doomsayers. Such an attitude will make the couple angry and move them into defensiveness.

The mentors' task is to help cohabiting couples become aware of their unique risks and help them deal with these problems. The Mentor Couple's role is to offer hope and encouragement. There is still time to remedy the special problems facing the couple. Mentors should assure couples, "We are committed to helping you work on these issues." The mission of mentors is to show couples what they need to work on and to discuss with them some of the problems caused by their cohabitation.

If You Want a Lasting Marriage, You Must Prepare Properly

Following are four essential elements of rigorous marriage preparation:

1. Objectively Identifying and Addressing the Strengths and Weaknesses of a Relationship

Every couple can benefit from an objective view of their strengths as a couple and areas of disagreement so they can address and resolve them—before the wedding. Perhaps the most reliable method for accomplishing this is by having each individual take a premarital inventory. Such an inventory raises more than 150 issues that offer the couple a comprehensive understanding of their relationship. Couples are asked if they agree or disagree with one-sentence statements such as the following:

- At times I am concerned about the silent treatment I get from my future spouse.
- Some relatives or friends have concerns about our getting married.
- I am concerned that my future spouse spends money foolishly.

2. Involvement with Positive Marital Role Models

Many individuals have never seen a stable marriage up close, so they can't begin to know what to aim for or how to make it happen. Mentor Couples are an invaluable model of a healthy marriage. They can help couples talk through their inventory responses and learn how to deal with differences and conflict. Potential mentors can be recruited and trained in any church.

3. Building Skills

Mentor Couples can teach premarital couples the necessary skills of communication and conflict resolution. Meeting every other week for four to six months, couples complete a series of exercises. They share their family of origin's style of problem solving, prepare a budget, and set personal and joint goals.

In addition, mentors encourage couples to move apart if they are cohabiting and ask them to consider remaining chaste until the wedding. By moving apart and practicing abstinence, the couple learns self-imposed discipline in the relationship.

4. DEVELOPING AND STRENGTHENING A RELATIONSHIP WITH GOD

Couples learn how to bring God into their relationship as a third partner. As Scripture puts it, "A cord of three strands is not quickly broken" (Ecclesiastes 4:12).

For the unmarried sexually active, this means returning to chastity. It's an essential component for premarital couples to receive God's blessing.

Couples also need to know how to nurture their faith. A husband and wife who have an active faith life will find it much easier to follow the scriptural admonition: "Submit to one another out of reverence for Christ" (Ephesians 5:21).

Couples who go through this four-step process not only can enter into marriage prepared but also can have a 95 percent chance at a lasting marriage.

HOW MARRIAGE SAVERS PREPARES COUPLES FOR MARRIAGE

When Harriet and I were asked to lead marriage preparation at Fourth Presbyterian Church in Bethesda, Maryland, in 1992, the program consisted of six lectures and a workbook. We added the elements of premarital inventory and couple mentoring, making it one of the first programs in the country in which trained Mentor Couples, as opposed to clergy or counselors, talked through the results of a couple's inventory and taught relationship skills. The course comprised four parts:

1. Premarital inventory (such as PREPARE or FOCCUS);
2. Mentoring (five to seven sessions to review all inventory items and relational exercises);
3. Lectures on marriage (given by experts and clergy); and
4. Workbook (teaching scriptural principles of marriage, completed by couples).

Let's consider these four components in more detail:

1. Premarital Inventory

Couples deserve an objective assessment of their relational strengths and challenges. This cannot be accomplished without a premarital inventory. Studies of two major inventories indicate that one tenth of couples who complete an inventory decide *not* to marry, to delay, or to cancel their wedding. "Couples who delayed were very similar to those who later got divorced and very different from those that were happily married. This indicates that couples who cancelled their marriage made a good choice because they would have had a high probability of ending up being unhappily married," wrote Blaine Fowers in "Predicting Marital Success and Divorce Using PREPARE."[5] The inventory helps couples avoid a bad marriage before it begins.

The most widely used inventory is called FOCCUS,[6] which according to its authors is taken by about 500,000 couples annually. PREPARE[7] is given to about 250,000 couples, and other smaller inventories, such as Zoë, are used by about 50,000 couples. However, 1.5 million of 2.3 million who marry have *not* benefited from such an experience.

FOCCUS and PREPARE inventories bring to the surface issues that confront all marriages—communication, conflict resolution, finances, parenting, sex, etc. These categories are covered in one-sentence statements to which each partner responds. Inventory authors recommend that partners be seated in separate rooms to avoid consulting on answers. Responses are scored by computer and summarized in a detailed report provided to facilitators, comparing what the man and woman answered on each item. The 2007 cost for computer processing is twenty dollars for FOCCUS and thirty-five dollars for PREPARE (fees are lower if the inventories are taken online or in volume). Scores are given based on the percentage of positive couple agreements in each relationship category.

The inventory provides an "X-ray" of the couple's current relationship, revealing strengths as well as areas where growth is needed. As one Mentor Couple observed, "It almost always identifies the problem areas in the relationship."

An inventory accomplishes two goals. First, it provides an objective assessment of a couple's current strengths and challenges—what one mentoree referred to as "the fundamental fact-finding part, in which you find out more about yourself and about your fiancé." Second, it promotes dialogue and encourages conversation. The inventory is an invaluable tool that helps couples air every issue. One young man, now happily married, said that it created a "good environment . . . to not shy away [from discussing issues] even if you wanted to."

Does an inventory evoke honest responses? Yes, because the statements call for responses about the other partner's attitudes, not about the individual completing the inventory. For example: "My future spouse is often unhappy" (FOCCUS); "Jealousy is an issue in our relationship" (PREPARE). If an individual is concerned about an issue, he or she is given an opportunity to discuss it in a safe, structured environment. Harriet and I have mentored couples using both inventories and have always felt that couples responded truthfully.

What Does a Premarital Inventory Look Like?

Examples from FOCCUS:

- I would like to change some of the ways we solve problems.
- There are qualities of my future spouse that I do not respect.
- My future spouse is a good listener.
- I am concerned that I am marrying too soon.
- The use of some drug (alcohol/tobacco/marijuana/cocaine) causes problems between us.

Examples from PREPARE:

- My partner sometimes makes comments that put me down.
- I am comfortable talking with my partner about sexual issues.
- In our marriage the husband should be as willing to adjust as the wife.
- I wish my partner were more willing to share his/her feelings with me.
- We have a specific plan for how much money we can spend each month.

2. Mentoring

By 1992 about 100,000 engaged couples a year were taking a premarital inventory administered by a pastor or a therapist, followed by approximately an hour of feedback. Typically, out of more than 150 items covered in the inventory, only three areas of strength and three areas of growth were discussed. However, Harriet and I strongly believed that couples would benefit from discussing *all* inventory items. Furthermore, we felt that dialogue should be facilitated by a seasoned married couple who could serve as their mentors. Such couples are a great untapped resource in every church: mature couples in healthy marriages who have time and wisdom to share with young couples. We piloted such a process with three initial couples in the spring of 1992.

That fall we were asked to lead marriage preparation at Fourth Presbyterian. We agreed on two conditions. First, that we could train enough Mentor Couples to administer the inventory and devote five or six sessions with each of thirty couples preparing for marriage each year. That would ensure time to review every item on the inventory. Second, that couples getting married at the church be required to take the inventory.[8] Fourth Presbyterian agreed to both conditions.

The mentoring process adds another sort of "test" to the marriage preparation process. It provides a way to tap the wisdom of older couples about how to resolve issues that seem impossibly complex to younger couples. Mentors have the time and experience to help couples discuss relationship issues thoroughly. Mentors serve not only as facilitators, prompting dialogue between young couples, but also as marriage models, demonstrating healthy roles and attitudes of husbands and wives.

By our adding the component of Mentor Couples to premarital preparation, the percentage of couples considering marriage in our church who chose to break up nearly doubled, from 10 percent of those simply taking an inventory in 1992 to 19 percent. (The average church, without an inventory or mentors, sees perhaps 1 percent of couples deciding not to marry.) More important, most couples strengthened their relationship as they addressed their unique challenges with the guiding wisdom and care of a successfully married couple.

This way of testing the relationship is far healthier than cohabiting, which usually leads either to the emotionally wrenching experience of a breakup before marriage—a "premarital divorce"—or a legal divorce after the wedding.

My 1993 book, *Marriage Savers,* was the first to describe the value of an inventory administered by mentors versus professionals. It helped spark a major increase in churches offering a premarital inventory. Numbers rose from about 100,000 couples taking an inventory in 1993 to about 800,000 in 2006. (That still represents only slightly more than a third of 2.3 million couples preparing for marriage.)

3. Lectures on Marriage

In addition to meeting with mentors to discuss an inventory, Fourth Presbyterian requires premarital couples to attend seven lectures on core relational marriage topics. For years, each week one key issue was covered: communication, conflict resolution, finances, marriage as a covenant, sex in marriage, and the importance of the marriage vows. Initially experts in the church gave the lectures: a financial planner would talk about money, a therapist would discuss listening skills, and so on. However, from 1998 to 2007, Dr. Glen Knecht, then pastor of Care and Counseling, taught all marriage classes from a biblical perspective.[9]

Several lectures were inspired by *The Mystery of Marriage* by Mike Mason. The book debunks the myth that marriage is founded on love. As Knecht and Mason have pointed out, though we do not enter marriage without love, once that step is taken and commitments are made, lasting marriages are founded on the *vows*: "for better or for worse, for richer or for poorer, in sickness and in health, to love and to cherish, till death do we part." Knecht also observed that healthy marriages are based on the commitment to remain together even when feelings of love may not be present.

In another lecture in his series, "Spiritual Foundations of Marriage," Knecht explained how marriage makes war with one's "single mentality"—that marriage is actually "dying to self," a sacrificing of the freedom of one's singleness. This spiritual foundation of marriage is reflected in Scripture: "As iron sharpens iron, so one man sharpens another" (Proverbs 27:17).

4. The Workbook

Completing a workbook is yet another component of the premarital program at Fourth Presbyterian. Two workbooks are used at our church: *Before You Say "I Do"* by H. Norman Wright and Wes Roberts, and *Before You Remarry: A Guide to Successful Remarriage* by H. Norman Wright. Couples are assigned chapters coinciding with the subject of weekly lectures. The workbooks ask couples to look up scriptures relating to key relational issues and to share their responses privately with each other as homework assignments. Couples learn the "mind of God" on major marital issues.

One engaged woman shared: "The workbook was a wonderful way to bring the true nature of marriage to the forefront."

A BETTER WAY TO TEST THE RELATIONSHIP

It *is* possible for a couple considering marriage to test their relationship in an appropriate way. By completing a rigorous premarital process, they can heed the apostle Paul's admonition "Test everything. Hold on to the good. Avoid every kind of evil" (1 Thessalonians 5:21–22).

The marriage preparation process is a helpful test. Yet, as we explain to couples, an inventory is not a test they'll pass or fail. Rather, it's an assessment or survey of a couple's current relationship. The inventory may indicate that a couple scored poorly on finances; however, the low score may only mean that in the glow of romance they haven't yet discussed money issues. The mentoring process takes place in a safe and confidential setting so couples can talk through a variety of relational matters, ranging from a decision to have a joint checking account to whether the woman wants to stay at home to raise children. As the couples talk through their inventory issues, they typically come to consensus before a matter becomes heated and difficult to resolve. Sometimes couples discover an issue that was lurking below the surface—such as one partner's unvoiced decision not to have children. An inventory helps to put on the table all issues couples need to discuss before marrying.

Fortunately, about 800,000 couples marrying today are given premarital inventories. Pastors who currently use an inventory need only train Mentor Couples in their congregations to administer it (as well as to teach conflict-resolution skills). Then a couple preparing for marriage can be matched with a couple who has time and a heart for investing in their future.

CHAPTER 8
Mentors and Mentoring

Command and teach these things . . . set an example for the
believers in speech, in life, in love, in faith and in purity.

1 Timothy 4:11–12

Our mentoring experience has been wonderful!! Our mentor
couple was very skillful and demonstrated tremendous pa-
tience and wisdom in sharing with us and in helping us to talk
through the issues in our relationship. We learned a lot from
them. We bonded with them right from the beginning and are
extremely comfortable with them and would be very comfortable coming back to them in the future to discuss issues or
problems that arise.

Tim, speaking of marriage mentors Victor and Patti Llewellan

THE VALUE OF mentoring is best expressed by the mentored couples.
Here's what Cheryl said of mentors Mike and Peggy Mader: "Our
Mentor Couple is a blessing from God. They have been skillful in help-
ing us. They are open and vulnerable with us to help us understand
how they resolve issues. They are also very attentive to the voice of the
Holy Spirit in attempting to help us. They have wonderful hearts."

Mentoring engaged couples is an important and effective strategy
for churches wishing to promote healthy marriages. But could the
process be made even more effective by intervening even earlier, before couples had committed to wed? We believe so.

Prior to Fourth Presbyterian's marriage preparation program using
Mentor Couples, all of the couples participating were engaged. How-

ever, as Lead Mentors, Harriet and I trained enough Mentor Couples to invite seriously dating couples to participate as well. With increasing numbers of couples cohabiting before marriage, we believed the church should take action early, providing an alternative—a better way to test the relationship before an engagement.

Increasingly, couples enrolling for premarital preparation were living together, claiming they were "testing the relationship." We provided them with evidence from both Scripture and sociology that shows the risks of cohabitation. We explained that moving apart is in the best interest of both the partners and the relationship, and encouraged them to do so.

By offering an inventory and a mature, wise couple with whom they could talk through issues, our church was providing a better, more biblical path for couples to test their relationship than living together.

Those taking a premarital inventory (which most mentorees call a "test") are indeed testing their relationship. Discussing results with a solidly married couple is an appropriate form of examination. And it's a vastly healthier way for couples to decide whether their relationship has the ingredients for a sound marriage.

Within a few years, about a third of Fourth Presbyterian's program participants were seriously dating couples. The classes grew from a dozen couples to twice that. Interestingly, most of the new couples came from outside the church. They had heard about the mentoring program from friends and business colleagues who had married at our church. Half were unchurched. We had inadvertently created a gentle form of evangelization!

THE PURPOSE AND PROCESS OF COUPLES MENTORING

The first step in the mentoring process is for couples, individually, to take an inventory that measures their behaviors, attitudes, and expectations about marriage and about their partner. According to Dr. Barbara Markey, creator of the FOCCUS inventory, "An inventory gives a premarital couple an opportunity to talk about things they didn't know they needed to talk about."

When Harriet and I mentor a couple, we have them sit in separate rooms while completing the inventory. Marking their responses to the 156 items takes less than an hour. The couple's answer sheets are mailed off to be scored by computer and returned in the form of an inventory report that compares how each responded to the statements.

In the case of FOCCUS, additional inventory items are included if either individual is remarrying, the couple is cohabiting, or if the pair has different religious backgrounds. This can bring the total up to 189 items. PREPARE has separate inventories for cohabiting couples and remarrying couples.

Mentors are encouraged to invite the mentoree couple to dinner for the first session, during which the two couples can become acquainted, and then administer the inventory. Sharing a meal is significant. It serves as an icebreaker. Dinner can be a relaxing opportunity for couples to meet in a social setting, as opposed to feeling like an appointment or a business meeting. Dinner reinforces the mentors' role as a caring couple who has no agenda other than wanting the mentoree couple to have a bright future—whatever that may mean.

The couple returns for at least five more biweekly sessions (usually over coffee and dessert), during which the Mentor Couple reviews with them every item on the inventory and administers the prescribed exercises.

Harriet and I coauthored, with Rudy and Faith Buettner, the *Mar-*

riage Savers Mentors' Guide, which provides a simple, step-by-step agenda for each session to discuss the inventory and to teach skills-building relationship exercises. These exercises help couples prepare a budget, learn communication tools, set goals, consider remaining chaste till the wedding, and moving apart if cohabiting. (If the couple is cohabiting or remarrying, an extra session is necessary.) The *Mentors' Guide* includes detailed suggestions on how to successfully address the sensitive issue of couples who are living together.[1]

A Bridge Across Generations

The premarital inventory creates a bridge across generations, revealing to the Mentor Couple specific issues the mentorees have identified as *their* challenges that need to be resolved.

The mentoring process gives trained married couples a rare opportunity, at a pivotal moment, to participate in the lives of another couple. It is a great privilege and honor.

This role also fulfills Scripture's call to "bear the 'burden' of being considerate of the doubts and fears of others" (Romans 15:2 *TLB*). Mentors can pass on to the next generation wisdom that made their marriage thrive and endure. It also offers an occasion to note mistakes that were made, letting mentorees know that a healthy marriage is imperfect but "under construction" and always in the process of improving.

The Benefits of Mentoring

Mentor Couples have three great gifts to offer a premarital couple:

First, they provide unconditional love, a love that grows out of the joy in their own marriage and out of gratitude to God for that blessing.

Second, Mentor Couples offer the gift of their own marriage—an imperfect but healthy example of a high-functioning relationship. They are role models, human parables of marital success and of pitfalls to be avoided. (Matching mentors and mentorees who have similar marital histories is vital. Initially, all of our Mentor Couples at Fourth Presbyterian were in primary marriages. But a third of mentoree couples involved remarriage by one or both partners who feared making another mistake. So we recruited mentors who had experienced a divorce but were in a stable remarriage.)

Third, they give their time. Mentor Couples typically spend two to two and a half hours each meeting with one couple for six sessions—seven if the couple is cohabiting, entering into a remarriage, or has a faith difference. Those twelve to twenty-one hours allow ample time to discuss issues in depth, a major investment of one couple in another without compensation. (By comparison, two-thirds of clergy offer no premarital inventory, and those who do typically allot only an hour to discuss it.)

The "premarital package" includes an appointment with the newlyweds six months to a year after the wedding. Married life has then become a reality. Mentors still have the couple's inventory to remind them of specific relational issues and can ask, for example, "Is he or she still giving you the silent treatment? Did he or she ever pay off all those credit cards as promised?" The message is that mentors are available if the couple has a need. As one of our mentors always said to mentorees, "Our porch light is always on for you."

That's a lavish investment of time for one couple to devote to another couple whom they typically do not know.[2] Why would they do it? Mentors feel that God has blessed them with a good marriage. They feel called to pass that blessing on to others.

With widespread divorce and the decline of the extended family, the wisdom and values of the older generation are no longer routinely passed on to the next generation. Many divorces are due to a lack of simple life skills that for one reason or another were not gleaned from parents and grandparents. One engaged woman remarked, "In our society there's usually some distancing. You don't know when to say things [to others]; you feel like you are intruding. But the mentors are given a license—the agreement up front is that they will get involved."

Training couples in healthy marriages to prepare other couples for marriage using an inventory was unknown when we began to do so in 1992. But it was successful from the beginning. As one mentoree put it, "You are our spiritual parents." One mentor, married for forty-six years, sagely told mentorees, "Before you tie the knot, let us show you the ropes!"

Studies of PREP, a marriage enrichment course developed at the University of Denver, indicate that clergy and lay leaders are as effective in teaching relational skills as psychologists and marriage professionals.[3] This is not surprising, because a lay couple can be open, sharing their successes and mistakes. Clergy and therapists, by contrast, maintain a professional distance and rarely share personal experiences. Mentors charge no fee, and they often bridge the generational gap to become friends. They are not mental health providers; they're relationship coaches.

Curiously, the need for marriage modeling in churches is more acute than is widely recognized. A Barna poll reported that "Christians are more likely to experience divorce than are non-Christians."[4]

Understandably, couples who marry in a church expect to have a greater chance of marital success. This misconception is widespread among pastors as well. The idea that those who marry in church are inoculated against divorce *can* be valid, but *only* if couples are adequately prepared. Taking a premarital inventory, with mentors acting as facilitators, and learning communication skills give couples what they need. This process requires organizing, training, and oversight by church and lay leaders.[5] However, it's a commitment that is worthwhile—and one that's called for in Scripture: to the Christians in

Philippi, Paul wrote, "Give more honor to others than to yourselves. Do not be interested only in your own life, but be interested in the lives of others" (Philippians 2:3–4, *NCV*).

The Issue of Time

One benefit of preparing and mentoring couples *before* they set a wedding date is the luxury of time. Couples who are seriously dating or engaged but have not set a wedding date tend to be more focused because they're not distracted by wedding plans and a deadline. One couple who broke their engagement three weeks before the wedding admitted, "We were trying to push the process with the Mentor Couple. We just had too little time." Sadly, sometimes the Mentor Couple feels as if they are competing with the wedding coordinator for the young couple's time. Often, the wedding coordinator takes precedence.

Yet according to Marriage Encounter, a weekend enrichment retreat attended by two million couples, "A wedding is but a day, and marriage is for a lifetime."

One mentor observed, "The couples that we helped the most were all seriously dating couples. The engaged couples were just too anxious to get it done. They just wanted to brush past any uncomfortable issues."

An engaged man expressed doubts to Harriet and me about marrying his fiancée. Privately he asked us for our opinion. We replied, "We never tell a couple whether they should or should not marry. That's for you to decide. However, since you are experiencing doubts, we recommend postponing the wedding until you've settled unresolved differences."[6] He dismissed our suggestion.

As the wedding date approached, he became increasingly apprehensive. Ultimately he broke the engagement—but only two weeks before the wedding. He'd already paid for the bride's parents to fly to the United States from Chile. The tickets were nonrefundable. But better a broken engagement than a broken marriage.

Time is an essential ingredient in making one of life's most important decisions. That's why we recommend that couples defer setting a firm wedding date until their marriage preparation is complete. Ideally, pastors should require a minimum of six months' time before the wedding.[7] The premarital counseling process requires at least three months, assuming the couple meets biweekly for six sessions. Some sessions inevitably get postponed, stretching the time to four or five months. If wedding invitations are already mailed, the pressure to marry is daunting, especially if doubts about marrying arise. No one should get married to avoid the embarrassment of a canceled engagement.

EXAMPLES OF THE MENTORING PROCESS

What is the mentoring experience like, using a premarital inventory?

ROBERT AND SUSAN are an attractive couple with advanced college degrees. She is a physician; he is an engineer. They met at an historic African-American church in downtown Washington, D.C. Since their church offered no marriage preparation, Susan phoned us to ask if they could come to our suburban church for marriage preparation. She added, "We love each other, but we are having trouble communicating. Can you help us?"

I said, "Sure. Harriet and I are both free, so we will mentor you ourselves."

However, when we received their inventory results, our hearts sank. They scored a zero on Communication and only 20 percent on Conflict Resolution.

An inventory can predict with 80 percent accuracy who will divorce, and this couple's scores were predictive of divorce. However, they are *predictive,* not *determinative.* What matters is how the couple responds to the issues raised. (We would never tell a couple that their scores predict divorce, because as Dr. David Olson, author of the PRE-PARE premartial inventory, once told me, "You don't know what a given couple's response will be to the scores. Will they work harder at their relationship or give up? That decision should be up to them, not to a counselor or Mentor Couple.")

Robert and Susan did show 90 percent agreement on Religion. Both were committed Baptists. I began by saying, "You scored high on issues of faith. Obviously, you both are committed believers. This is an important strength in your relationship."

Harriet added, "Your faith can be a bridge over troubled waters. When you have a problem, you can pray for God's wisdom."

I added, "Yes, but you do have some troubled waters under that bridge. For example, you apparently both give each other the silent treatment. Susan, give me an example."

She responded by telling a story: "A few weeks ago, we were going to Robert's friend's house for dinner. He said he knew how to get there, but he didn't. We drove in circles. We passed a gas station, and I suggested, 'Why don't you call your friend and ask him where he lives?' Robert retorted, 'I know where he lives. I've been there.' Then we drove around for another half hour and finally arrived an hour late. I was so angry that I didn't call him for two weeks. He was so embarrassed that he didn't call me, either."

I turned to Robert and said, "You should have gotten directions in the first place. Or, when it was clear you could not remember where your friend lived, you could have taken Susan's suggestion and called for directions at the gas station. What you did was childish. You let your pride get in the way. You didn't even apologize when you were an hour late. The relationship is *always* more important than the issue.

When you do something like this, you should apologize. If you had, your relationship might have gotten stronger. Instead, you stopped communicating for two weeks.

"Now, Susan, on another issue, you indicate that Robert does not share his feelings with you."

"That's right," she responded.

I noted that on another item, Robert said Susan did not understand him. I said, "Well, this is a 'two-fer,' Robert: if you share your feelings with Susan, she *will* understand you. But you don't. She can't. Now, let's say she called you at the end of the day and said, 'How was your day?' What would you say?"

He replied, "Oh, I might say it was terrible or great or something."

I shook my head, "Bad answer. Women want detail." (Harriet and Susan laughed.) "You need to say something like this: 'My day was terrible. I lost two days' worth of work on the computer.' Or, 'It was great because I got a compliment from my boss.'"

Susan's face lit up as she said, "That's it! That's the stuff he never tells me."

Harriet chimed in: "Robert, you *can* say more than you think she needs to know."

Two weeks later, when we saw them for the next feedback session, they seemed happier. I asked, "How's it going?"

Susan said, "Great!"

"Has Robert been sharing his feelings with you?"

She nodded enthusiastically. "Yes! Miracle of miracles!"

I asked Robert, "Do you feel better understood now?"

He brightened and said, "Yes, and she's not nagging anymore!"

"How about the silent treatment?" I asked.

Robert laughed. "Oh we haven't done that since you said it was childish."

We were delighted. We reviewed the rest of the Communications and Conflict Resolutions items with them again, and to my astonishment, they scored 100 percent on both!

Now, I have to confess, this was one of quickest turnarounds we had ever seen. We simply asked common sense questions based on what Robert and Susan had told us about themselves. Any couple who has been married twenty to forty years could do this with ease.

Still, the enormous maturing of this couple is something we have often witnessed while mentoring. Their growth is proof that inventory scores are only *predictive* of problems—*not determinative*. What matters is not the test scores but whether the couple wants to work at the relationship and learn how to resolve the problems that have been brought to light.

LILLY AND DUANE had excellent scores on their inventory. They were dating seriously but not yet engaged. Neither had ever been married, though she was forty and he forty-one. However, when they came to the issue of children, Lilly exclaimed to her mentors and Duane, "I can't wait to have my first child. I want to have one right away."

Duane was shocked: "I told you we are not going to have any children. I'm forty-one. I don't want to be putting kids through college when I am ready to retire."

Hurt and dismayed, Lilly lamented, "But marriage means children."

Her boyfriend shook his head: "Not to me it doesn't."

Her voice grew weaker. "But I thought you'd change your mind after we were married."

Growing angry, Duane snapped, "My love for you should be enough. I don't want to share your love with anyone else!"

Lilly and Duane broke off their relationship. Although they'd had high scores predicting a healthy marriage, an inventory cannot measure the depth of feeling on any one issue. They had an irreconcilable difference. Fortunately, however, they discovered it in time—before they were married.

DOROTHY AND JIM had dated in college but moved on. Neither married. They met each other again years later, when they were around forty, and came to us for mentoring. When the results of their inventory came back, I was crestfallen. The scores were all 20 percent or lower (scores predictive of a future divorce). I was careful to show no trace of my concern when I called Dorothy. "We have your inventory report and are ready to have you come over to discuss it."

"Oh, Mike, never mind," she quickly replied. "I broke our engagement."

Surprised, I asked, "What prompted you to break up before you even met with us?"

"When we left your house after taking the inventory, we talked for three hours. I asked him how he answered the questions. We were poles apart on everything! I said to Jim, 'You know, we're going to have to go back to Mike and Harriet's and talk about this.' He barked, 'No. I am not going back there!' When I asked him why not, he said, 'I don't want these strangers asking us about our personal life. I don't know them. It is none of their business.'"

Dorothy said at that point she took off her engagement ring and handed it to him, sadly saying, "Then this engagement is broken."

Jim was dumbfounded: "You're breaking our engagement over some stupid piece of paper?"

Wisely, Dorothy replied, "No. I'm breaking this engagement because you're not willing to work at this relationship. If you won't do so now, when you say you love me, what hope do I have that you will do so after the wedding?"

Dorothy already had qualms about becoming engaged; she admitted to me that she and Jim had communication problems. But at age forty, she feared not finding anyone else. The good news is that a year later, a widowed physician proposed to her. Today they are happily married, and she took on an instant family of two children.

What if she had not taken a premarital inventory and had married Jim? She might well have experienced the pain of divorce. A study of PREPARE indicated that couples who break their engagements have the same scores as those who marry and later divorce. Mentors and couples should view broken engagements not as failures but as divorces avoided.

HAROLD AND ANGELA each had been married previously. They dated each other for *eight years,* unable to decide whether to marry. Things would be fine for a while, but then there would be an explosion and a cessation of dating for months, followed by another cycle of dating and breaking up.

With their marital background, it was important to match Harold and Angela with a couple who had experienced a failed marriage. Couples in primary marriages are best suited to work with couples preparing for marriage for the first time. Those who have divorced but successfully remarried are better equipped to mentor those considering remarriages. Consequently, we paired Harold and Angela with Harry and Carolyn Lincoln, who, in spite of previous failed marriages, had enjoyed a solid twenty-five-year marriage to each other.

Harry asked Angela and Harold this question: "Have you shared why your previous marriages failed and what your role was in their failure?"

Harold had, but Angela had not. She explained, "I was married at age twenty and divorced at twenty-one. I had no children. The details don't matter."

"They *do* matter," Harry insisted. "Tell us your story."

As it turned out, Angela had buried her feelings so deeply that she was unaware that when she and Harold began considering marriage, she became fearful and pulled away, throwing sand in the gears of the relationship. Once she understood what she was doing and why, she was able to build the relationship into a lasting marriage.

Had their mentors not experienced failed marriages themselves, they may not have understood the issues confronting this couple.

THE EFFECTS OF MENTORING

JoAnna, who (with her fiancé) met with Ron and Marge Beukema at our church, said this about their mentoring: "This was the best part of marriage preparation. Although we have talked about a lot of things on our own, it was helpful to discuss them with someone else, especially someone besides our parents. They [Ron and Marge] were also a wonderful example, especially for someone like me who comes from a broken home. We learned a lot about working together and compromise from them."

Of the fifty-six couples Harriet and I have mentored, nine decided not to marry—the exact same percentage of breakups experienced by our church. Of those couples, one discovered, as a result of taking the inventory, that they had so few relationship strengths that they broke up without meeting with us again.

One young couple, who had dated since high school, quarreled over many matters and took our advice to postpone their wedding twice. They later realized theirs was not a marriageable relationship. They broke their engagement and eventually married more suitable partners.

Another couple broke up when the woman discovered that her boyfriend was addicted to pornography and was unwilling to enroll in a course to help him address the addiction.

In every breakup, it was the couple who decided not to marry. As mentors, we did not reveal our personal opinions but made it clear that the decision to marry was theirs and theirs alone.[8]

Of the forty-seven couples we mentored over fifteen years who did marry, we know of no divorces (although one couple is in crisis). And the success is far broader than just that witnessed by Harriet and me. In 2001 Catherine Latimer, a Marriage Savers intern, conducted a survey of 302 couples who had registered for marriage preparation at Fourth Presbyterian between 1992 and 2000, when Harriet and I were the Lead Mentor Couple. (During that time we trained fifty-three Mentor Couples to administer a premarital inventory and relational exercises.) Following is Catherine's summary of the 302 mentorees over a decade, as of September 2001:

- Fourteen couples could not be located.
- Twenty-one couples dropped out of the program, mostly to break up; one eloped, two changed churches.
- Thirty-four couples completed the course but broke off their relationship or engagement before a wedding could take place.
- 222 couples completed the process, married, and are still married.
- Five couples married and divorced; two married and separated.
- Three couples were still engaged and scheduled to marry in 2001, while two were dating but considering marriage in 2001, and one couple was being mentored.

You'll notice that brings the total to 304. Two couples were counted twice: one broke up and later reunited and married; another broke their engagement but were still dating.

Thus, fifty-five couples either dropped out because they broke up or completed the process and decided not marry. That's 19 percent (of the 288 couples with known results) who decided not to marry. But these breakups do not represent failures. They are success stories—individuals coming to mature and difficult decisions from a well-informed point of view. Better a broken engagement than a broken marriage with children. In fact, as noted earlier, studies of PREPARE found that those who decided not to marry after taking a premarital inventory had the same scores as those who married and later divorced.[9]

The fifty-five couples who did not marry avoided a bad marriage.

Of the 222 who married, only 7 divorces or separations took place in a decade. That's only a 3 percent failure rate, or a 97 percent success rate over a decade. This is more than marriage preparation. It's *marriage insurance*.[10]

Compare those results with the odds that a couple living together will have a marriage that lasts ten years: 16 to 20 percent. Adequate marriage preparation reverses those odds.

To put it differently, couples who have a *"prepared"* marriage (one that was preceded by a premarital inventory and relationship exercises administered by a Mentor Couple) can achieve a *lifelong* marriage. The evidence is overwhelming that having trained Mentor Couples available to administer a premarital inventory and talk through the issues that surface is incredibly helpful in preparing couples for marital success. The biggest problem is that few churches have trained Mentor Couples.

In light of these facts, some questions need to be asked:

- If you are cohabiting, wouldn't you like to have a fulfilling, lifelong marriage?
- If you are a parent of an adult child who is cohabiting, why not suggest he or she seek a lifelong marriage instead?

- If you are in a solid marriage, why not suggest to your pastor that your church become a Marriage Savers congregation and offer to be a Mentor Couple?
- If you are a pastor or church leader, why not create a program proven to promote successful marriages?

THE IMPORTANCE AND ROLE OF MENTOR COUPLES

Administering a premarital inventory creates an opportunity to add a second important element in building a lifelong marriage: tapping the wisdom of an older couple in a healthy relationship. Catholics often call these couples Sponsor Couples. Protestants use the term Mentor Couples.

In traditional marriage preparation programs, an inventory is administered by a clergy person or therapist. Pastors and priests have limited time to go over results. Typically, they review the couple's inventory in just an hour. Few of the 150 or more items can be addressed in so short a time. Even so, merely taking the inventory and discussing a minimal number of responses prompts one tenth of couples to decide not to marry.

However, we believe it's beneficial for a young couple to test their relationship more thoroughly by meeting with a trained Mentor Couple who has the time and heart to discuss with them their responses to *all* of the inventory items. That's why we train mentors to administer the inventory and then meet for five or six additional feedback sessions, each of which is two or two and a half hours long. That gives couples a ten to fifteen times longer investment than can be offered by most clergy.

With the added component of Mentor Couples, instead of 10 percent of couples deciding not to marry, nearly twice as many—19 percent—broke off their relationships. However, of those who do marry, *the divorce rate drops to only 3 percent over a decade.*

The core reform Harriet and I created in our premarital program is the Mentor Couple. Harriet and I trained our first dozen Mentor Couples in 1992. We have since trained sixty-six couples in our home church and about four thousand Mentor Couples in fifteen hundred congregations. Those trained mentors (and clergy) have since trained others. Years after we trained those first couples, I articulated this foundational principle in *A Manual to Create a Marriage Savers Congregation:* **"In every church and synagogue there are couples with strong, vibrant marriages who could be of help to other couples but have never been asked, inspired, or trained to come alongside another couple and be helpful."** [11]

It's time to bring this resource out of dormancy and start asking strong couples to invest their married lives where they'll make a significant difference—in the lives of couples just getting started.

When we invite couples to consider mentoring, almost all are reluctant. They feel unqualified. Their first reaction usually is, "But I've never studied psychology" or, "We don't have a perfect marriage." We overcome that hurdle by showing them that the resources we provide make it simple for lay people to facilitate meaningful dialogue. The included follow-up questions in the FOCCUS inventory help probe an issue. Some mentors find that they don't even feel the need to refer to them; however, they have an extra measure of confidence knowing that those questions are available for reference if they get stuck.

Mentors hold the *Facilitator Notebook* on their laps like an insurance policy that guarantees they do a good mentoring job. The *FOCCUS Facilitator Notebook* and our *Marriage Savers Mentors' Guide* allay any fears. When we were training a group in which everyone present had only a high school education or less, I heard one truck driver exclaim exultantly to his wife, a waitress, "We *can do* this."

All that's required of potential mentors is what they already have—

experience and wisdom—along with a heart for helping others build strong marriages. A Mentor Couple's wisdom about marriage can be a priceless gift to the next generation.

MARITAL INVENTORY FOR MENTORS

How can a church be certain that a potential Mentor Couple has a healthy marriage? When we served as a Lead Mentor Couple for our church, we administered as part of the training an inventory for married couples called REFOCCUS. This tool reveals the DNA of the couple's relationship. Later we invited each couple to our home for dinner and a private discussion of their inventory results. In about one-tenth of the cases, they decided—or we concluded—that their marriage was not strong enough at that time for them to be mentors. That's why, during training, we always refer to the trainees as *potential* Mentor Couples, giving both the couple and the church freedom to back away.

Although REFOCCUS is intended for marital enrichment, it serves as a useful tool for assessing the marital health of a candidate Mentor Couple. Unlike FOCCUS, the premarital inventory, REFOCCUS is self-scoring and so inexpensive (ten dollars) that churches can afford to give every couple a copy of it during training. Harriet and I have led marriage enrichment weekend retreats using REFOCCUS in churches on a Friday night and Saturday guided by the *REFOCCUS Manual for Extended Use,* which can be ordered from FOCCUS, Inc. After such a weekend, here were typical reactions from attendees:

- "It gave us hope and a plan to restore what we were losing."
- "The inventory allowed us to speak about things we

never realized had such an impact on our lives, and I
learned a lot about myself."

- "This weekend helped me come to understanding my
  wife better."
- "We were able to discuss a painful event without
  argument."

The REFOCCUS marital inventory can benefit couples at every
stage of married life. See pages 187–188 for more details on using
REFOCCUS as an enrichment tool.

Rewards of Mentoring

Why do Mentor Couples volunteer their time without pay? Mentors
are motivated to serve because they are grateful that God has blessed
them with a solid marriage and want to pass on the significance that
faith has had in their marriage. Because they're recruited from
churches, their faith is important to the discussion of Religion and
Marriage Covenant—two key categories in the FOCCUS premarital
inventory.

Mentor Couples find their own marriages are enhanced through
the process as well. As Jesus said, "Give, and it will be given to you"
(Luke 6:38).

One mentor, Deborah, called Harriet several years ago to say that
she and her husband couldn't take on any more couples. "Please remove us from the list. My mother broke her hip and has moved in
with us."

But six months later, Deborah called again: "Please give us another couple to mentor."

Harriet was surprised. "Oh, your mother healed quickly!"

"No," she explained. "But our own marriage has gotten rusty. It
was much more vibrant when we were mentoring. Scripture says, 'Iron

sharpens iron.' When we focus on another couple's relationship, we inevitably focus on our own."

A PASTOR'S VIEW OF MENTORING

Rev. Jeffrey Meyers[12] of Christ Lutheran Church is one of the first pastors in the United States to create a Marriage Savers Congregation that has virtually eliminated divorce. His church of 1,500 has had few divorces since 1996. He wrote a "Pastor's View of Mentoring" for *A Manual to Create a Marriage Savers Congregation:*

> What does the typical couple look like that enters the pastor's study for marriage? As a pastor I shudder when I stop and ponder the answer to the question. The typical couple is already sexually active. Most likely they are living together or at least planning on living together before they get married. They will cite economic reasons for living together. They may cite convenience as another reason. Many will live together to see if they are sexually compatible but will never tell the pastor that.
>
> This typical couple will bring at least one divorce into this marriage relationship. They probably began dating before the ink dried on the divorce decree. This typical couple will bring at least one child from at least one other relationship. Half of the children that go through one divorce will face another before they reach the age of 18.
>
> This typical couple will come into the pastor's office convinced that they are in love and have learned from their previous mistakes. They are convinced that they share a spiritual relationship where God has brought

them together. After all, anything that feels this good must have God's blessing.

Most pastors face this scenario repeatedly every year. "What can I do?" many of us ask. "Do I encourage them to marry quickly to make it 'right?'" *Honestly, since when does a wedding solve a sin problem?* But the time constraints of a busy ministry schedule make it very difficult to give the attention and guidance that most couples need as they prepare for marriage. Some pastors will wisely administer a relationship inventory and walk the couple through the results. This is good, but can more be done? Who follows up after the wedding when so many troubles begin within the first year of marriage?

Perhaps the biggest tragedy is that most churches and pastors choose to do nothing. By doing nothing, this typical couple will be divorced within five years. The children of this and previous unions will face another family breakup. Failure in marriage, another broken family and more parental desertion will cut deep scars of insecurity, loss, anger and a shattered identity in the lives of these children.

Yet sitting in the pews and chairs of our churches are strong, committed and capable couples who have been married three or four decades. Before our eyes Sunday after Sunday are couples who have learned the secrets of building a fulfilling marriage. These couples are waiting to be asked to help.

When I realized the potential of the securely married couples in my congregation, I recruited them, trained them to administer an inventory, and equipped them to meet with another couple through the first year of marriage. It took some time. A weekend training and some monthly meetings. But I soon realized that there were couples willing to lead a team of Mentor Couples. So really, after the first three couples were trained we formed a marriage preparation team. The engaged couple was referred to this team and I met with the engaged couple once or twice as the wedding approached.

What happened was amazing. First of all, my workload diminished after the first Mentor team was trained. Second, we began to do a much more thorough job in preparing couples. Third, couples were involved in hands-on ministry. In the mentoring process we were adding value to marriage as a congregation. More people were involved in making marriages succeed.

Then my Mentor Couples began to report what difference mentoring was making in their lives. This was a ministry they could do together. Mentoring pulled their families together around a meaningful service to others. So much of what they do in church sends the family in splintered directions, and mentoring pulls them together. The couples that they mentored began to talk about being mentored as a transforming experience. These couples felt prepared for marriage and secure in their decision to marry. I also noticed that the number of those choosing not to marry increased.

The biggest success is in watching the Mentor Couples share Jesus Christ with the couples getting married. They spend time praying with these couples, modeling a life of discipleship as a family to a couple open to answers at a crucial time of life.

Now when a couple comes into my study something has changed. Sure the same typical couples come through my door, but what we do has changed. Now I have a new confidence, secure in what a team of Mentor Couples can do to help them build a lifelong marriage. I know that when this couple walks down the aisle and they share vows together, they will look at each other with confidence having learned from a success story,[13] Reverend Meyers concluded.

Mentoring matters! Few opportunities exist in which individuals can intervene in the lives of others and make a significant difference. But mentoring offers just such an opportunity. Mentoring a cohabiting couple to help them prepare for marriage the right way will give them the gift of a bright, stable future and a secure family environment in which their children can grow—indeed, thrive.

CHAPTER 9

Teaching Relationship Skills Hector and Teresa: A Case Study in Mentoring

Whatever you have learned or received or heard from me, or seen in me—put it into practice. And the God of peace will be with you.

Philippians 4:9

We had issues we could not resolve. . . . I felt we could talk through a lot of things with the two of you. . . . We looked forward to coming to your house for mentoring. That helped us set our sights on something higher.

Hector, referring to the success of his and Teresa's mentoring sessions

THE PRIMARY FUNCTION of Mentor Couples is to act as relationship coaches who support and encourage mentorees while teaching skills of conflict resolution and equipping couples with the effective tools—for communication, budgeting, and goal setting. Mentors both model and teach marriage skills, walking alongside premarital couples as they seek to upgrade their interpersonal skills and make their future marriage a success.

The goals of mentoring, as stated in the *Marriage Savers Mentors' Guide*, are to:

- facilitate dialogue on issues surfaced in the FOCCUS inventory;
- model and help develop healthy communication skills;
- encourage couples to find *their* solutions to *their* problems;
- help premarital couples share family heritage, prepare a budget, and set goals;
- encourage the couple's spiritual growth; and
- share personal marital wisdom.[1]

This sounds like a tall order—and it is—but the *Mentors' Guide* makes it easy. The nineteen exercises in the guide are designed to help premarital couples learn and apply all the important relationship skills they'll need for their upcoming marriage. It's the best kind of teaching—not by lecture but by experience—the kind of teaching that lasts.

With the help of the premarital inventory and the *Mentors' Guide*, Mentor Couples assist premarital couples as they work through their unique differences. They help mentorees learn how to listen and how to express thoughts and feelings openly and with respect for their partner.

What follows is a case study—an example—of the mentoring process in action. Through it you can see the effective techniques used, get a taste for the valuable resource the *Mentors' Guide* can be, and get comfortable with the mentoring process and some of the issues you might encounter as mentors, especially if your couple is cohabiting.

A COHABITING COUPLE WHO SOUGHT PREMARITAL PREPARATION

"Hector" and "Teresa" registered for our church's premarital program, and Harriet and I were assigned to be their mentors. They are African American, have master's degrees, and are successful in their respective careers. Hector was working as a top assistant in a major federal agency. He earned $75,000 annually, an excellent salary for a young man of thirty. Teresa, twenty-nine, was a federal consultant and earned $70,000. They heard about our church's premarital program from friends.[2]

Hector and Teresa's crossing racial and cultural lines and traveling a long distance to our home to be mentored demonstrated a commitment to the program. Since they were living together and we were writing this book, I asked permission to take notes and share their story (provided we changed their names and allowed them to read our draft for accuracy). They readily agreed.

At our first meeting they appeared to be a happy couple, bubbling with stories about how they'd met. Hector was an extrovert, enjoying people and parties. Teresa was an introvert.

"I'm the last one in my group of friends to get married," Teresa said with a sigh. "I'm so thankful I waited, because I see a lot of unhappy marriages, some with adultery."

"We've had our ups and downs," Hector admitted. "It has been a growing process."

Teresa thanked us for agreeing to mentor them, adding, "I want to get married only once. So I want to make sure we're doing it right."

WHY COHABIT?

When they told us they were cohabiting, I asked why.

Hector had moved into Teresa's apartment six months before the wedding, and they later purchased a townhouse. He explained, "We have to save money. We're paying for our own wedding. One monthly payment is lower than two rents. Also, the lease expired on my apartment, so we decided to buy a home now—stop paying rent and share a mortgage. We're putting money into our pockets rather than giving it to the owner of the apartment building."

Teresa perceived moving into their townhouse as a step toward peace. "I hated my apartment, which was noisy. Many tenants played loud music. We have a future together—let's get started."

For Hector, as with most men, living together was an economic move. I suspected that sexual accessibility was another, unvoiced reason, as it often is.

I asked how they reconciled their faith, which prompted them to attend church weekly, with cohabitation. He replied that since sex was already part of their relationship, he felt that they were already married—all they needed was the paper to make it legal.

Teresa demurred softly, "It's a source of religious guilt for me."

WHY MARRY IN A CHURCH?

"Why do you want to marry in a church?" is the question asked in Exercise 18 of the *Marriage Savers Mentors' Guide* for cohabiting couples.

"I want to get married in a church," Hector explained. "It's very important to me to have a religious ceremony." Teresa remained silent.

I made a case for their moving apart, saying, "Couples who marry after living together are fifty percent more likely to divorce. Are you willing to move apart until the wedding?"

"No," Hector declared firmly. "We will not move apart."

Teresa concurred. "It hasn't even crossed my mind."

"I can't afford another mortgage," Hector added. "And we have to pay for the wedding."

"No one is suggesting that you buy a second house," I explained. "I'm suggesting that one of you move out and live with friends until the wedding. Might you consider the more biblical way? You are Christians who worship together. Secular psychologists and statisticians have arrived at the same conclusion as the church: that cohabitation is harmful. We want you to succeed.

"Whether you move apart or not, we will teach you relationship skills, like how to resolve conflict. But because we care about your future, we urge you to consider moving apart. No single step could do more to increase your odds of a lifelong marriage. Will you reconsider?"

The couple shook their heads.

Objectives of Exercise 18: Cohabiting Couples

The *Marriage Savers Mentors' Guide* provides exercises to address three special issues: interfaith marriages, remarriage, and cohabiting couples. Exercise 18, which is shown here, addresses the following objectives:

- Bring a positive approach to the couple's desire to build a healthy marriage.
- Inform the couple of risks associated with cohabitation and help them identify which of these risks may apply to them.

- Deal directly but constructively with issues putting their relationship at risk.
- Encourage the couple to articulate their thoughts about their living arrangements.
- Have the couple consider the benefits of moving apart until the wedding.

THE OPTIONAL PREMARITAL SEXUAL COVENANT

It seemed futile to broach the topic of an Optional Premarital Sexual Covenant, since the couple was living together. However, I forged ahead.

I read from Paul's letter to the Thessalonians that couples should avoid "sexual immorality" and that "each of you should learn to control his body in a way that is holy and honorable, not in passionate lust like the heathen, who do not know God" (1 Thessalonians 4:3–5).

Data from Exercise 3

Divorced/ Years of Marriage	Divorced/ Separated Virgins	Divorced/ Separated Non-Virgins	Percent Higher
1980–1983	14% (by 1988)	24% (by 1988)	71%
1975–1979	21%	34%	62%
1970–1974	30%	46%	53%
1965–1969	30%	50%	67%

I showed the couple data from Exercise 3 indicating that couples who marry as virgins are much less likely to divorce than those who are sexually active. "You have a choice," I said. "You can't be a virgin again, but you can decide to remain chaste until the wedding. You would reduce your odds of divorce if you played by God's rules. Are you willing to do so?"

They said nothing.

"We're not asking for a decision tonight. Think about it and pray about it. If you are not going to move apart, there is a way you could live under the same roof, but biblically." I introduced the Optional Premarital Sexual Covenant. "Of course, the sexual temptation when still living together would be great—which is why we still strongly recommend that you live separately.

Optional Premarital Sexual Covenant

The *Marriage Savers Mentors' Guide*'s Exercise 3 encourages couples to remain or become chaste. Couples are provided with compelling and practical biblical, statistical, and sociological evidence that sexual activity before marriage is harmful. The covenant urges couples to act on this new knowledge by signing a pledge to refrain from sex until after the wedding.

The Optional Premarital Sexual Covenant

What is outlined below is a voluntary pledge by a seriously dating or engaged couple to chastity. It is optional, but is strongly encouraged. Secular research provides evidence that couples who live by scriptural standards are far more likely to have a lifelong marriage. Therefore, your Mentor Couple will ask you to consider limiting your physical involvement, as indicated below, and to be accountable to your Mentors. The goal is to build a relationship on a foundation that can last for life. Premarital couples are asked by their Mentors at their second session to discuss the Covenant privately among themselves, to pray about it, before deciding whether to take this step. Regardless of what your decision is, the matter will remain a confidential one and will not affect your continuing in the premarital program. Ultimately, it is a spiritual matter between you and God. The purpose of the Covenant is to support you and help you to be accountable to the pledge.

1. Be honest about the physical part of your relationship. Consider making a commitment to keeping your physical level at #7 or below.

(1) Look	(6) Strong kiss
(2) Touch	(7) **French kiss**
(3) Lightly holding hands	(8) Fondling breasts
(4) Constantly holding hands	(9) Fondling sexual organs
(5) Light kiss	(10) Sexual intercourse

2. If the physical level exceeds #7, you must both be willing to inform your Mentor Couple. The Mentors' role is to help you get back on track without being judgmental. The man must contact the male Mentor within 24 hours after exceeding the physical limit. If the man does not do so, the woman will call the female Mentor. Being

(continued)

accountable to your Mentors keeps your focus on spiritual, character-building issues, which are important in forming a lifelong, committed marriage.

We pledge to hold our conduct to a biblical standard so the Lord might bless this relationship now and in the years ahead. Therefore, we agree to call our Mentors if our physical involvement goes beyond level #7.

Couple   **Mentors**

_____   _____

_____   _____

                                          Phone No. _____

Date: _____   Date: _____

"You don't *have* to sign this covenant, but we do *ask* you to consider signing it. Because we think it's so important, we will bring up the matter again. However, we'll continue to mentor you, regardless of your decision."

ECONOMIC ISSUES

We asked Hector and Teresa how they made financial decisions.

Hector replied, "We agreed we would buy new cars, and I bought a new car first."

But Teresa was unhappy that he'd made the decision unilaterally. She interjected, "He likes to process stuff internally. If we had processed it together, there might have been a different decision."

Exercises: Finances and Budgeting

Marriage Savers created two exercises on finances and budgeting for mentorees to complete. The first, Exercise 5, is designed for partners to track their spending for a month. The second, Exercise 11, asks couples to prepare a monthly budget together and gives helpful basic guidelines as to what percentage of income should reasonably be allocated for various expenditures. It also points out the following red flags that indicate an individual or a couple is in financial straits:

1. For the past six months you have paid all basic living expenses with a credit card.
2. You pay only the minimum amount due each month.
3. You have more than one credit card.

She clearly felt she had to give in on the car. I encouraged them to consider Ephesians 5:21, which says, "Submit to one another out of reverence for Christ." I explained that in a good marriage, no one makes unilateral financial decisions; they are made jointly. "Hector, when you bought the new car, you probably thought, 'I earned this money. I should be able to decide for myself how to spend it.'"

He nodded. "That's right."

"However," I countered, "the money you spent on the car means there's less money for your wedding, your honeymoon, or furniture."

Hector answered, "As far as our home is concerned, we've contributed equally. We earn evenly. The utilities are in my name, but we each pay half of the electric, for example. The townhouse is in both names."

Teresa dissented: "He has chosen to keep our finances separate.

Maintaining separate checking accounts is a common pattern among cohabiting couples. They don't trust each other, knowing the partner could leave at any time. Consequently, protecting one's assets is important.

We're not making decisions together on what benefits a family. There hasn't been much communication. We have a joint account to pay household expenses, but we maintain separate accounts. It concerns me."

Hector sidestepped the issue, rationalizing, "If I have bills, they're my responsibility. If there are things that I want to do or that she wants to do, we should have that right. It's not a question of a nest egg on the side." He had said earlier that his father had a separate account for his body shop work, which Hector apparently thought was fine.

Harriet pointed out, "You're living as if you were independent people. Marriage is about interdependence. A joint checking account means accountability. It builds oneness."

Hector stood his ground. "We are very fiscally responsible, both of us. We're in agreement about how we'll make decisions." Yet he then acknowledged, "We have not yet come to an agreement. We're still discussing."

WHAT DOES LOVING SOMEONE MEAN?

This had been a painful, difficult session, covering cohabitation, chastity, and financial conflict. Therefore, we concluded the evening by giving the couple an uplifting exercise: Exercise 4, Affirming Love. I read, "Think about what love means in the context of your relationship with your future spouse and answer this question: 'What does loving someone mean?'"

They both wrote for ten minutes and shared warm words of love.

Teresa wrote eloquently: "Love is a decision. It is not an emotion. Loving someone means I have made the decision to let you into my life, into my personal space. Love means accepting that person for who he is and not trying to change him. It means I have to lay down personal pride or the need to win. We will work for a harmonious future."

Hector wrote: "Affirming love is a selflessness, going above and beyond because you care. It is investing in tomorrow. It is educating your partner on your history and life. It means being friends. Love is patient and endures a lifetime. Love brought both of us to this situation, and it will take us beyond the horizon."

Despite their earlier sense of anguish, they reconnected and practically floated out of our home.

That was our goal, because no couple *has* to return to continue being mentored. Yet every couple has come back for additional sessions (though not all completed the full number of sessions).

CONTROL AND TRUST ISSUES

When we met two weeks later, Hector and Teresa were in conflict over many issues. Selfishness reigned. For example, Teresa would not cook his dinner, retorting, "I'm not your wife." She explained to us, "He expects me to cook a meal each night. I'm just his girlfriend. When I come home, I am tired, too. He asks, 'Where is my dinner?' and I say, 'I'm eating cereal. If you want a hot meal, you cook it. We're not married.'"

Another inventory item states: "I am concerned that one factor may dominate our life together." Teresa answered yes, that she agreed with that statement. Asked about it, she put it in one word: "Work."

Hector acknowledged, "I'm very career oriented. I have a lot of aspirations. I plan to run for office one day—perhaps U.S. Senator. It will take a lot of my time. I do balance work and home. However, in my field there are many social events where I meet with people I work with. She needs to understand this is part of my work."

That subject brought another issue to the surface. On Hector's thirtieth birthday, he had a party and invited a number of coworkers, including two "young ladies," as he put it. One of them then invited Hector to dinner.

Hector defended himself: "I didn't want to go out with these young ladies by myself. I asked Teresa to join us, but she refused. I work with them every day. For me it's just a business meeting."

Teresa snapped, "Whether it's business or social, it's someone of the opposite sex. I met one of them before the party, and I didn't like her."

"You're trying to control my friends and who I go out with," Hector said angrily. He turned to us and grimly announced, "She's not helping me with my career."

"He has a lot of lunches with girls," Teresa said. "I'm not totally comfortable with that. When I call and say, 'Let's have lunch,' he often has other plans. So I ask, 'Who is she?' So when I heard he was planning dinner with two of them, I was uneasy."

"It comes down to trust," Hector said. "She doesn't trust me."

Harriet spoke up: "Trust is the foundation of a marriage. You shouldn't do anything to erode it. It can eat away at someone's heart. However, when a hurting partner complains about something like this, sometimes it inadvertently comes across as nagging or controlling.

"Many of the issues you fight over would likely disappear if you lived apart. If one of you won't move out of the home, you could sleep in separate bedrooms until your wedding day," she suggested. "Chastity honors God. I'm convinced such a step would give your relationship a line in the sand, a new beginning. Marriage should be a defining moment, a new beginning of life for both of you. After all, you'll have to practice chastity with everyone outside your marriage for the rest of your life. Can you be chaste with each other for the five months until the wedding?"

Two weeks later, while Hector and Teresa were on their way to our home, a female colleague called Hector on his cell phone and invited him to dinner. To the disbelief of his fiancée, who was sitting next to him in the car, he accepted. Baffled by her anger, he sought my approval.

He argued, "I've told Teresa she could come to dinner with us. She doesn't want to join us. So what's the problem?"

"The problem is that you are engaged," I replied. "You can't accept a date from another woman. You have to cancel that dinner date. You must realize that you are unavailable to other women."

Hector responded defensively, "I'm not interested in her."

"She's interested in *you*. And you think you're *still available* because you are not yet married. That's why you accepted her invitation."

IN-LAWS AND OTHER CONFLICTS

That evening another sensitive issue surfaced. Hector, and his mother, wanted his sister to be a bridesmaid. But Teresa didn't like his sister and had already chosen five close college friends to stand up with her. This was not an issue until his mother asked him to let his sister be a bridesmaid.

"Teresa says it is her wedding, so I'm going to let her do what she wants to do," he said, looking at her. Then he turned to us. "I would prefer that we had worked it out to accommodate my sister."

Apparently, when Hector brought Teresa home to meet his family, things were said that resulted in hurt feelings. Teresa told us, "Now when his mother phones, she always calls on his cell phone, never on the house phone, and she never speaks to me."

"You need to do something positive," Harriet commented, "and you're running out of time. I think you need to communicate to your future mother-in-law that you love Hector and appreciate the parents who gave you this wonderful man. Perhaps you could write her a letter. There's something nice about a letter; you can choose your words carefully."

Hector loved that suggestion and urged Teresa to do so.

Teresa resisted. "I don't have time at work to breathe."

Harriet again tried to mediate: "Her [the mother's] anger is an expression of her hurt. You don't want her to stew. Pray about this. You might say, 'God, you love these people, and you know them far better than I do. Give me a loving heart toward them.' Let God change your heart and hers."

Teresa explained further: "At times he has made up his mind with me, but then he talks to his mom and changes his mind."

Hector acknowledged that while he sided with his wife, "I didn't totally agree on five bridesmaids. I knew the impact of her decision on my sister. My mom says she wants my sister as a bridesmaid. That was the one thing I wanted in the wedding."

I asked, "Why not have six bridesmaids?"

Teresa muttered morosely, "If I were to ask her now, would she do it? I don't think so. She told me, 'I don't want to have anything to do with your wedding.'" In a burst of anguished emotion, she added, "Last week I was coordinating the entire wedding. I had to find bridesmaid dresses that ranged in size from two to twenty-two in matching colors. But Hector had not even finalized his guest list and given me a count of his invitees. In addition to having to get all of this stuff done, I hate my job, and the situation with his family is miserable. It ruins the whole engagement experience. He says, 'Why are you complaining when you have only a few things to do that are time sensitive.' " She burst into tears and blurted out, "I don't feel like dealing with this."

Hector tried to change the subject. "Why are we talking about this and not talking about the sister situation?" It was the wrong thing to say.

Teresa raised her voice in despair. "The whole process is so miserable, I'm thinking about canceling the wedding. I'm sick and tired of fighting with him on too many battles. Everything has been going wrong from the beginning. I want to be done with it. I want to be happy with something in my life. Nothing is good right now."

Harriet and I were stunned. We both wondered, *Why is this couple even considering marriage?* As Harriet observed after they left, "They don't seem to even like each other, let alone love each other."

We introduced them to an exercise called the PREP Speaker-Listener Technique, a communication skill that could help them to resolve conflicts. We asked Teresa to summarize her position on the bridesmaid issue using this technique.

The PREP Speaker-Listener Technique

This communication technique, developed at the University of Denver by Drs. Howard Markman, Susan Blumberg, and Scott Stanley,[3] is designed to clarify an issue, increase listening skills, and offer opportunities for problem solving.

Both the Speaker and the Listener must abide by certain rules called "the Floor." The Speaker may bring up an issue, but must be succinct stating it, so that the Listener

(continued)

---

can paraphrase what has been said. The Speaker must use "I" statements rather than "you" statements to avoid sounding accusatory. The Listener may not respond substantively, while the Speaker has "the Floor." The Listener may paraphrase what the Speaker said, to be sure that it was correctly heard. The Floor doesn't change hands when the Listener is responding. The Speaker can keep "the Floor" as long as he/she feels the point of view has not been fully expressed or heard correctly. Then the Speaker gives "the Floor" to the Listener, and the Speaker becomes the Listener, and the Listener becomes the Speaker, changing roles and repeating the process to seek understanding.

We asked Teresa to summarize her position on the bridesmaid issue.

Teresa (Speaker): "There is a lot of stress in planning this wedding. It would mean a lot to me if the issue about our family's participation were not pushed right now."

Hector (Listener) paraphrased.

Teresa (Speaker): "The way you are handling the family relationships makes me question whether the relationship is worth it. I feel like I am forced to do things the way *you* want me to do things, on *your* timetable."

Hector (Listener) paraphrased, summarizing, "So for you it is creating a burden on the relationship?"

Teresa (Speaker): "When I am forced into a corner, I feel like I have to fight back."

Hector, now shaken, became the Speaker and replied, "I am not sure how the relationship will survive the next big issue. I have some doubts about how strong we are and whether we are staying together. If we cannot resolve the family situation, it will impact future decisions."

Teresa (Listener) paraphrased and explained, "It is more about how we handle it, how we think about it. There is too much unnecessary pressure."

Hector began to realize that he needed to remove some of the pressure and take responsibility: "I realize I need to make things right."

Teresa became the Speaker, and began to calm down, saying, "I sense that when I get additional responsibilities, I don't respond quickly, and you get upset. Sometimes you act like I am a child."

Soothingly, Hector repeated the essence of what she said and added, "I've been too harsh or critical of the work you are doing."

She murmured quietly, "I need your support."

We felt they had made progress and were ready for the next exercise. We taught them another technique, a Step-by-Step Plan for Solving Problems.

THE STEP-BY-STEP PLAN FOR SOLVING PROBLEMS

We wanted to give Hector and Teresa another communication skill for their "tool box." The benefits of this particular exercise are many. The Plan provides a structured format. The first step makes it possible for the couple to mutually agree on a time they will discuss the problem. That gives both partners an opportunity to reflect on the issue before they meet, as well as the confidence that it will be discussed. Describing the problem in writing promotes deeper thinking than

simply conversing about the issue. Having to identify how each partner contributes to the problem encourages both to take responsibility
for the issue, giving the relationship balance. Listing possible solutions places the focus on finding constructive answers to the problem
instead of playing the blame game. The inclusion of prayer and forgiveness as steps offers a spiritual intimacy in the midst of discussing
differences. The Plan ensures a win-win result.

When the couple used this technique to help with the family issue,
Hector prayed, "Lord, thank you for allowing us to deal with this dif-

Exercise: A Step-by-Step Plan for Solving Problems

1. Choose a time when both of you can concentrate on the problem.
2. Describe the problem.
3. Pray together for God's guidance.
4. Indicate how *you* have contributed to the problem.
5. List attempted solutions that failed.
6. Brainstorm. Write down possible new solutions.
7. Take turns reading aloud solutions to try from each list.
8. Mutually agree on solutions to try from each list. Be specific about what each of you intends to do.
9. Forgive each other for the pain this issue has caused.
10. Schedule a time in the next few weeks to assess progress each of you has made toward solving the problem. If the problem is not resolved to each person's satisfaction, return to Step 6 and try other solutions. Set a date to discuss your progress.

ficult situation. Help us to develop solutions and to walk away from this with one heart."

Teresa prayed, "God, remove the bitterness and anger from our hearts. Keep us strong and positive so that when trouble comes, we look to you for guidance. Help us to grow."

PROBLEM SOLVING VERSUS "THE LAST MAN STANDING WINS"

By the opening of our next session, the couple seemed happier. The conflict-resolution tools we had given them to use in discussing difficult issues had enabled them to make some breakthroughs.

However, when they took their premarital inventory, both Hector and Teresa had agreed with this statement: "I would like to change the way we solve problems." We asked what they would like to change.

Teresa replied, "One thing I do not like is one person walking away when they don't want to talk about it. I suggest we have a ground rule that allows a person to take a time-out, but then the issue should be revisited. They can come back with a cooler temper. I would like us to be nicer when we argue."

"I don't like to talk about a situation too long," Hector explained. "I'll walk away when I feel the time limit is up. She wants to continue to talk about it. I give her the silent treatment; then she gives me the silent treatment. This is counterproductive."

This issue exemplified a classic gender difference: women tend to bring up a problem and want to talk it through to resolution in a detailed fashion, while men tire of hearing the women repeating their points, and they shut down.

The greatest cultural gap in America is not between races but between genders. Failing to understand gender differences, both the man and the woman think the other is being unreasonable. The average man speaks thirteen thousand words a day, the average woman twenty-three thousand. Both have to compromise—the man talking more than he'd like, and the woman less than she would prefer.

Hector said, "I feel like we're both trying to build up a case why we're right rather than figuring out what the problem is. She has an independence, a determination. I want to be heard, and I want to be right."

Teresa agreed: "We never want to fold the tent."

Harriet observed, "You sound like two lawyers trying to win a case instead of two people who love each other and are about to be married. What issues do you argue about?"

Hector put it succinctly: "My independence versus hers. I remember her nagging me about something—like that I didn't clean up. The argument was exhausting. It erodes the relationship and eats away at you. She always has to win."

Teresa spoke quietly: "Yes, but I feel that I'm always giving in."

"So how can you negotiate a win-win situation?" Hector asked. "That's what I do at work all the time. We concentrate on team building, coalition building. At work, emotions are not involved. It's a win for me and for everyone."

"You need to find new ways to resolve conflict," I suggested.

Hector continued: "Our arguments are over trivial stuff. She puts me down, criticizes how I clean up. She puts the garbage in the trash can, and I carry it out. But she complains that I don't put a new bag in the trash can.[4] Yet she doesn't recognize when I do something special. I put up a shelf for her, and she says it's not straight. That irks me."

Harriet read another item from the inventory: "I am satisfied with the way my future spouse expresses his or her feelings of disapproval or anger."

Hector answered, "I agree."

But Teresa shook her head. "I'm not satisfied. He uses mean words. We need to be kind—even in anger. If I say, 'You didn't clean up the kitchen,' he does part of the job and then will come back with something negative about me. It's like a boxing match. You poke him, and he pokes you back."

"So the last man standing wins?" I asked.

Hector's response, directed at Teresa, was harsh: "I'm sorry that sometimes when I say something it comes out sarcastic. I'm sorry you're hurt. But if you're hurt, it's your problem."

I read the next inventory item and was disturbed to hear the answer: "The behavior of my future spouse sometimes frightens me." Teresa nodded gravely. I asked, "Has he ever hit you?"

"He grabs a lot." She turned to Hector and said, "One day at your apartment, we got into a pushing match. You pushed me, and I said, 'I will not let you push me.'"

Hector defended himself: "She started it. I let her push me. I stopped her from what she was doing. It did turn into a pushing match. But it only happened one time."

Harriet interjected, "One time is enough. That kind of behavior can escalate."

I warned Teresa, "Couples who live together are three times more likely to be physically abusive than a married couple.[5] Why does this happen? Cohabiting couples are not married—they haven't made a lifelong commitment to one another. Because they're unmarried, they're not fully invested in the relationship. They think more in terms of what their *individual* interests are rather than what's in the best interest of the *relationship*. They tell themselves, 'I don't have to put up with this.' It's too easy to get out."

SECOND THOUGHTS ABOUT MARRIAGE

When Hector and Teresa next came to see us, they were depressed. He had just received an unwanted job reassignment. She was increasingly unhappy with the relationship and told us, "I can't think about living the rest of our lives together. I feel anger, resentment, and negative feelings that are close to the surface," she complained. "When we started the relationship, I wanted to be with Hector. But he always fights for what he wants. I'm sick of being the person who has to give in. I feel like I have to defend myself all the time. We're always butting heads.

She added, "I also hate my job. He says, 'We have a mortgage to pay.' If I were to quit my job today, the impact would be dramatic. It's all about the finances. It's not about being happy."

Hector replied, "Let's live on one income for a while. We're talking about having children—"

"I don't want to bring children into this," Teresa interrupted. "I don't see how these issues will be resolved."

I added another dose of reality. "The best thing for each of you may not be each other. Nine of the forty-eight couples Harriet and I have mentored [up to that time] decided not to marry. Harriet and I agreed with their decisions—although we never shared that with them."

While Harriet and I did indeed privately wonder whether Hector and Teresa could work things out, we encouraged them to take several steps:

1. Attend an "Engaged Encounter" the next weekend.
2. Reconsider moving apart.
3. Remain chaste until the wedding.

Harriet explained, "If you distance yourselves physically until the wedding, you'll discover new power from the Lord in your relationship. When you discontinue sex, you'll be able to see more clearly what you're walking into."

A few nights later, Teresa made an anguished phone call to us. She was in tears, so upset that she had a hard time speaking. "I'm ready to break our engagement," she said. She seemed bone tired. She hated her job, and wedding planning seemed pointless if she didn't want to spend her life with Hector—who was unaware she was calling us.

Harriet tried to soothe her. "I understand how you feel. But these decisions are best made when you have a cool head. You're scheduled to go to the Engaged Encounter in two days. You've already made a deposit. I suggest that you go. This would be an opportunity, in a structured environment, to talk about all these issues that are so upsetting."

A MAJOR BREAKTHROUGH AT THE ENGAGED ENCOUNTER

Only six days after Teresa told us that she didn't think she could go through with the wedding, she and Hector were exultant about their relationship after attending an Engaged Encounter.

"The Engaged Encounter weekend was perfect for us," reported an ecstatic Teresa. "We were completely focused on one another. There were sixteen sessions. The first three to four are focused on communication. Then we did finances, and then forgiveness, which was the last one. It was perfect."

Hector agreed. "It was very beneficial. They were committed to making sure these engagements work and made it clear what you're getting into when you get married."

Harriet underscored one of the points they learned: "Love is not a feeling. It is a *decision*. Feelings are neither right nor wrong. They just are."

I read 1 Corinthians 13:4–6, adding, "There are fifteen definitions of love here, such as 'Love is patient.' None of these definitions is about feelings. Each requires an act of the *will*. Biblical love involves a *decision*."

One part of the weekend's discipline was for the couple to write each other a "love letter" for ten minutes on an assigned topic. They then went to a private area to read each other's letters and talk for ten minutes. Engaged Encounter and Marriage Encounter call such an exercise a "10 and 10."

Teresa said that when they started writing love letters, "We found we were saying the same things on paper to each other, such as my staying home with the kids. We had argued about that, but I learned in his letters that he was okay with my staying home for two to three years."

Harriet and I warmly congratulated them both—first for going to Engaged Encounter, and second for developing a new consensus on how to make their marriage work. This was a major breakthrough. All of the conversations we'd had with the couple on this issue seemed to have planted seeds that sprouted at the Engaged Encounter.

The Engaged Encounter that Hector and Teresa attended was sponsored by the Mennonite Brethren, who separate the men from the women, housing them in separate dormitories. We asked the couple what they perceived as the value of requiring them to remain chaste during the weekend.

"We were able to work through some issues which had been problems for us," Teresa said. "It was like I loved this boy and could not be happy without him. But there were a lot of things each of us was holding onto—clashing. As we followed the rules of the weekend (such as remaining chaste), we were able to focus on each other more clearly and intensely. We decided to leave our negative thoughts behind, issues that were not beneficial to our relationship."

Without sex confusing the issue, the couple said they were able to truly focus on each other. This is exactly what we had been encouraging them to do, and why. When they experienced mandatory chastity over the weekend, they came to understand the value of the discipline.

Harriet and I were thrilled by this new evidence of the power of

God in Teresa's life. I asked, "Why is having a set of religious values important—honoring God and living by his laws?"

"That's what life is all about," Teresa replied. "We're going to sign the agreement that we'll remain chaste until the wedding!" (The wedding was then three months away.)

I turned to Hector. "Do you agree with this?"

"I respect her decision on this. It's up to her. I don't feel as strongly as she does."

I persisted, "What is the value of chastity from your perspective?"

"The value for me is that there is now peace."

Teresa added, "I knew I was doing wrong. Now my conscience isn't bothering me. I would use sex as a weapon. I was taking it away from him when we got into fights. Now we can focus on the real issues."

How Many Sign the Covenant?

Of the forty-seven couples Harriet and I have mentored who were not chaste when they began the program, forty-three chose to sign the Optional Premarital Sexual Covenant. All of those who remained chaste agreed that their communication greatly improved and their respect for each other was enhanced.

Why did such a high percentage agree to follow biblical norms? I think it's the data proving that chastity pays dividends, as illustrated by the chart on the Optional Premarital Sexual Covenant reported on page 153. That significantly increased odds of a lifelong marriage.

Harriet congratulated them and predicted, "Signing the covenant will make a night-and-day difference in your relationship."

And that's exactly what happened.

THE NEW RELATIONSHIP

The next time we saw the couple, their relationship had been transformed into one of mutual respect and love that's typical of a premarital couple. Although they still faced problems with Hector's family, for the first time in our months of meeting with the couple, they seemed to be in agreement. They were on the same team.

While on the Engaged Encounter weekend, Teresa finally wrote a letter to Hector's mother—something we had encouraged weeks earlier.

She shared with us what she had written: "This engagement started out on a bad foot. However, you and I are two people who both care about Hector. Although I am receiving joy from him, I know our relationship has given you pain. I want to find ways to remove that pain. I want a comfortable relationship with you as family."

Hector smiled as he watched his fiancée reading and added, "It took a lot for Teresa to take that step. She has done her part. That's all I wanted. I'm proud of her for writing the letter."

Harriet asked him, "How did your mother react? Was she appreciative?"

"She was surprised," he replied. "It's hard for her to let me go. It will take time for her to accept it fully. When I talked to her, I said, 'Did you get the letter? I tried to get the two of you to talk. If you love me as much as you say you do, I would look forward to your honoring my marriage, by reaching out to me and to my wife.'"

His mother's response was not encouraging; she was still resentful that Hector's sister would not be in the wedding. So Hector went to his father and asserted, "We're going to talk this out, man to man. My mom and my sister are not where they should be on this marriage."

As he reported this to us, I watched Teresa. She was beaming as she listened to the account of her future husband coming to her defense.

THE VALUE OF CHASTITY

One of the inventory categories is Sexuality Issues. On the item "I am concerned that either my future spouse or I may use sex as a way to control each other," Hector said, somewhat acerbically, "She's over that now." In other words, it had been a problem before they decided to remain chaste. But now that they were not having sex, it wasn't an issue.

"There are advantages in remaining chaste," Teresa acknowledged. "I had a guilty conscience when we were sexually active. I'm a lot more at peace now about our relationship. I also greatly anticipate our wedding night."

"I can't look that far ahead," Hector said with a laugh. "It's too far away."

I asked Hector how he viewed the advantages and disadvantages of abstaining from sex. "The disadvantage is, it's tough to wait. The advantage is that she's much happier. It has been a concern of hers. It's one less issue that we argue about. Another level of anger is taken away."

"How do you feel it has helped you as a couple, now that you can't rely on sex as a bonder to restore intimacy? Has your communication improved? Do you feel that abstaining from sex has made you more able to express yourselves verbally? Have you found other forms of intimacy? Are you more affectionate?"

Teresa said, "Not having guilt feelings has taken away a layer of issues between us. I can be more affectionate. We take more time to cuddle. I feel more like when he was courting me. And we spend more time talking. We're growing together as a couple. I need that intimacy."

Hector shook his head, clearly not agreeing that the lack of sex made them closer. "It's a hard thing. I definitely do not think the lack of sex makes us closer." He had said before that he considered himself married to Teresa, though the wedding had not yet taken place. Therefore, he felt deprived of what he saw as his natural right—even though they were not yet actually married.

Harriet interjected, "This is part of the problem of premarital sex. One thing both partners know about each other is that the person is sleeping with someone to whom he or she is not married. This can be the beginning of questioning a partner's fidelity. It can plant a seed of doubt. If sex outside marriage has happened before the wedding, what might happen afterward?"

I added, "We men have to build barriers around ourselves. The most important sexual organ is the brain. To guard ourselves from temptation, we need to learn from what others do to practice fidelity. I once asked Billy Graham how he avoided sexual temptation. I knew that he once went to his hotel room after a rally and found a nude woman in his bed. Thereafter, he always had a staffer search his room before he entered it. However, he did more than that. He told me, 'I build a moat of protection around myself. I will not be alone in a room with a woman who is not my wife, nor will I ride alone in a car with my secretary, because it may cause some to speculate that we are having sex.'

"So by practicing chastity now, you are building a moat of protection around yourselves, building new trust in each other. If you can be chaste with one another now, when the temptation is greatest, that discipline will make it easier for you to remain chaste—not intimate with anyone *but* each other—after the wedding, when you might be tempted to stray."

Harriet added, "You want to make your relationship a sanctuary."

Teresa understood. "Infidelity starts before the situation occurs. It's a frame of mind, of always turning toward each other and not away," she said. "I have to turn away from all others who are not Hector. You don't put yourself in those tempting situations. That means there are no lunches with people of the opposite sex, no dinners, no hanging out. That's the plan." She spoke with a new sense of confidence we had not seen before.

Hector nodded in agreement. "I second everything she said. You can't turn to someone else. I don't want to have that as a route to take. It's no longer an issue. No more lunches or dinners with other women."

This was clearly a new Hector sitting before us. His acceptance of this limitation on his freedom clearly gave Teresa a new joy and hope for the relationship. It was exciting to witness.

THE COHABITATION TIMELINE

We gave the couple a new exercise, the Cohabitation Timeline. In doing so, I explained, "Three things are needed for a healthy marriage: respect, trust, and commitment. We can teach you communication tools, but if that rock-solid commitment isn't there, the tools are pointless.

"Although you may view your cohabitation as a committed relationship, commitment in marriage is very different. A successful marriage requires *permanent* commitment.

"We would like each of you to complete a timeline that graphs how your commitment has changed from the time you first began living together to the present." I handed each of them a page with a straight line across the middle. "Make a graph of your relationship. Using dates, events, problems, and turning points. Indicate the high

> # Exercise: Cohabitation Timeline
>
> Exercise 19 in the *Marriage Savers Mentors' Guide* helps cohabiting couples achieve the following goals:
>
> - See that their perceptions of commitment may not be the same.
> - Note how commitment may have changed during cohabitation.
> - Think about the meaning of commitment.
>
> Each partner charts his or her attitudes and level of commitment over the course of cohabitation, including dates, events, problems, and turning points. Graphs are then compared and discussed. It can be an eye-opening experience for couples.

points above the line, and low below, of the time you have lived together. Then share your thoughts with each other and with us."

The exercise was very revealing.

Teresa began her timeline the previous October. "I had a high when we moved in together in October. On Thanksgiving we had a big argument, so the line goes way down. In February we began having wedding issues and high pressure, which pushed the relationship to a new low through April. We bought a townhouse in mid-April, which was a low point, and my line goes below the chart. Then on Memorial Day he went to lunch with a female colleague, and that was another low point. After that he agreed not to go to lunch with any more women, which was a high. We signed the Optional Premarital

Sexual Covenant in August, which was a high point. At the Engaged Encounter, our relationship went higher. Today I hear Hector talking about being a 'new Hector,' and it's very high."

Next Hector shared the points on his graph. "I start with a high when we moved in together in October. We had a big argument, and Thanksgiving was a sad day. I went home to my family by myself. In December, I persuaded her to take this step of engagement. There was friction at our engagement party, which was on my birthday. It was the best party I ever had. My parents met Teresa on Memorial Day weekend. It went well but not as well as I'd hoped. I thought we were making strides, but Teresa was unhappy.

"In April we began the premarital course. I was determined, thinking, 'We need to make this work.' We had issues we could not resolve. She was not happy at all. We felt we could be open with you guys. By July, I felt we could talk through a lot of things with the two of you. The Engaged Encounter was even higher than my engagement. My line goes over the top of the paper. That helped push us over a major barrier, and we were more confident. We looked forward to coming to your house for mentoring. That helped us set our sights on something higher."

Then the couple exchanged graphs. Hector had recorded buying a home as a high. For Teresa it was a low point. We asked them to explain their thinking to each other.

Hector said, "In buying a home, I was staking a claim in the middle class. We had arrived. We had ceased being renters and instead were using monthly payments to put money into our own pockets as we paid off the townhouse."

Teresa explained, "For me that was not a happy situation. At the closing, his attorney said, 'This is the second home Hector has bought with a woman.' I was shocked. I learned only then that Hector had been engaged before, but it was called off. He had lived with another woman. They had bought a house together, but it didn't work out. The whole thing made me so sick that I didn't feel like moving in with him. In fact, he moved in weeks before I did. I remember thinking that this person, someone I had trusted, was not being truthful with me. I started questioning other aspects of our relationship. I thought, where do we go from here?"

Another high point for Hector was their engagement party. For Teresa, however, the event was a plateau moment, just a stop on the line in the middle of the page.

Hector was surprised. He turned to her and said, "To me, getting engaged to you was a high point. I had saved up for the ring, and I gave you a lovely party to announce our engagement. You had always wanted to be engaged. Why wasn't it a high point for you, too?"

"We were already living together," she replied. "The party was more for you than for me. It was male ego." She turned to us, adding, "He brought his future wife to introduce to his friends. The engagement was not a new stage of the relationship, just a mark along its course. I felt no different afterward."[6] She turned back to Hector. "And you throw parties all the time. This time you were just showing me off to your friends."

Hector sighed deeply.

That led her to add something that must have hurt him: "Hector doesn't want this engagement to end. It's a pride thing with him. He doesn't want two broken engagements." She continued, "It took time to rebuild trust again. From February through August, I didn't want to even look at the townhouse. That was a long time. I couldn't get out of the car. I didn't want to move in with my emotions as turbulent as they were. It took a while before I could go into that place and be happy about it."

SUMMARY OF HECTOR AND TERESA'S MENTORING

The historic Christian admonition—that sex belongs only within marriage—is wise counsel. From the beginning Teresa felt guilty about violating that rule. She knew that she was flouting centuries of biblical teaching. She felt she was building a relationship on shifting sand. When Hector pressed her to buy a home with him in April—months before their November wedding—she felt queasy about it. Then, when she learned at the closing that he had bought a house with a previous girlfriend, her unarticulated fear that he would be unfaithful was amplified. She could not bring herself to move in, though he had done so.

During their initial months of cohabitation, Hector had not made a full commitment to Teresa. He was lunching with other women so regularly that he was usually busy when Teresa called to make a luncheon date. He casually dismissed her repeated requests for his wedding list of guests. She was planning every other aspect of the wedding, and he could not even produce names and addresses of his friends and family.

For months during our mentoring sessions, the couple argued about so many issues that Harriet and I wondered why they were even considering marriage. It had become increasingly clear that Teresa's unhappiness was rooted in her fear that Hector would be unfaithful. That fear had a basis in reality. Finally, however, after Engaged Encounter, he acceded to her insistence that they remain chaste until the wedding.

Almost overnight their relationship changed for the better. He had earned her respect, and though he grumbled, he admired her high ideals. She began fixing lunches that he could eat at his desk, removing the temptation to lunch with women at work. He saw the value of that as a step toward building her trust in him.

When the couple remained chaste and learned a new communication skill of writing for ten minutes and talking for ten minutes at an Engaged Encounter, they discovered that the process prompted another major breakthrough. As Teresa put it, "It really helps me to see his point of view. I found myself saying, 'Oh! *That's* what you meant.' So now when we have an issue, I say, 'Before we start down that road and fight, let's do the "10 and 10" so we can see what the real issue is.' We use it as issues arise."

THE HONEYMOON

Hector and Teresa were married in November 2003 and honeymooned in the Caribbean. When they flew home, stopping in Miami to change planes, they called us from the airport. I picked up the phone, and Hector said, "Mike, get Harriet on the line." I called to Harriet, and she picked up another phone. Then we heard an astonishing thing.

"Mike and Harriet, we want to thank you for giving us a fabulous honeymoon!"

As if we had paid for it, when all we had done was to help them find the rock of Christ upon which they could build their marriage.

Although Teresa and Hector have had their share of rough spots over the years since their wedding, the mentoring process equipped them with the insights and tools they needed to successfully negotiate, communicate, solve problems, and relate to each other. Perhaps best of all, they had a support system in place—a committed Mentor Couple—to help them through future trials. In fact, the couple came to our house twice in their first three years of marriage, for help in talking through issues. Newlyweds—particularly those who have lived together prior to marriage—need to be able to count on a Mentor Couple for wisdom and support when they encounter problems. Hector and Teresa knew we would be available when they needed us.

The Community Marriage Policy®

My prayer is . . . that all of them may be one, Father, just as you are in me and I am in you.

John 17:20–21

Our concern as ministers of the gospel is to foster lasting marital unions under God and to establish successful spiritual families. Almost 90 percent of all marriages are performed by pastors, and we are troubled by the nearly 50 percent divorce rate. Our hope is to radically reduce the divorce rate among those married in area churches.

Excerpted from the Modesto Community Marriage Policy

January 1986

CHURCHES HAVE REASON, opportunity, and resources to make marriage a priority across an entire city, county, or metro area. If scores of churches together will follow the proven strategy outlined in this chapter and launch programs to prepare, enrich, and restore marriages, they can drive down both divorce and cohabitation rates and ultimately raise marriage rates.

Sound impossible?

It can be done. Indeed, it *has* been done by 10,000 pastors and priests who made a public commitment to marriage by signing a Community Marriage Policy®.[1] They pledged to prepare couples for lifelong marriage and also to fortify all marriages within the church using proven methods of enrichment and restoration.

"Faith is the assurance of things hoped for, the conviction of things not seen," wrote the author of Hebrews to a people who were being persecuted. This book was written with that same faith, in the hope that the next generation of believers will rebuild the institution of marriage to be what God intended it to be.

Living Together: Myths, Risks & Answers provides a detailed roadmap for the church to chart a new strategy of support for marriage, beginning with thorough marriage preparation administered by mentors. But a second step is also important: creating a Community Marriage Policy. In this step all participating churches in a local area agree not only to minimum standards of marriage preparation (a premarital inventory and four to six months of mentoring sessions) but also to a marriage-support strategy that includes enrichment of existing marriages, restoration of troubled ones, reconciliation of separated couples, and helping stepfamilies to be successful. (See Appendix A for a sample Community Marriage Policy.)

In January 1986, I persuaded ninety-five ministers in Modesto, California, to sign what I called a Community Marriage Policy, America's first clergy covenant. I predicted that if the clergy agreed to certain core reforms, their area's divorce rate would fall by 50 percent in five years. In 1989, *Christianity Today* reported that the divorce rate of Modesto (Stanislaus County) was indeed dropping. And by 2000, the rate had plunged by 50 percent. Interestingly, the number of marriages nearly doubled—from 1,300 in 1986 to 2,500 in 2005—in sharp contrast to the 50 percent national decline in U.S. marriages from 1970 to 2005. (We later learned that Community Marriage Policies had also reduced the cohabitation rate.)

As pastors heard about this progress as recounted in my book *Marriage Savers: Helping Your Friends and Family Avoid Divorce,* I received many invitations to help clergy groups create their own Community Marriage Policies (CMPs). In 1996, when fifty CMPs were in place, Harriet and I cofounded Marriage Savers to build a national CMP network, across denominational lines, to make marriage a priority in our nation's churches.

By August 2007 more than 10,000 pastors and priests had adopted 220 covenants in 44 states (see Appendix B) to help marriages at five key stages:

Stage 1: Before marriage, PREPARATION—Clergy agree to require four to six months of marriage preparation that includes (a) a premarital inventory to help couples assess their relationship and avoid bad marriages before they begin and (b) trained Mentor Couples who give "marriage insurance" to the engaged by discussing their inventory results and by teaching skills to resolve conflict along with key biblical principles for building a successful marriage.

Stage 2: During marriage, ENRICHMENT—Clergy pledge to conduct an annual retreat for married couples at the church at a low cost so that every couple can afford to attend.

Stage 3: After crisis, RESTORATION—Clergy commit to training "back-from-the-brink couples," whose marriages nearly failed but who are now in a state of healing, to Mentor Couples who are currently in crisis.

Stage 4: During separation, RECONCILIATION—Clergy promise to strive to restore separated couples by matching a support partner of the same gender with the spouse trying to save the marriage, using a proven and effective course called "Reconciling God's Way."

Stage 5: After remarriage, STEPFAMILY ASSISTANCE—Clergy agree to create Stepfamily Support Groups so couples in remarriages with children from a previous marriage can be successful parents and partners. Instead of losing 70 percent of such marriages to divorce, Stepfamily Support Groups save four out of five.

CHAPTER 10

WHAT ARE THE GOALS OF A COMMUNITY MARRIAGE POLICY?

In a Community Marriage Policy, a cross-section of local religious leaders from many denominations make a public covenant to prepare, enrich, and restore marriages in their congregations by helping couples achieve six great goals (the first two of which are detailed in this book):

Goal 1: Avoid Bad Marriages Before They Begin

Administer a premarital inventory to give couples an objective assessment of their relational strengths and areas for growth. Studies show that one-tenth of couples who take an inventory decide not to marry. Those who break an engagement after taking an inventory score about the same as those who marry and later divorce, indicating that such premarital breakups are actually helping couples avoid bad marriages before they start.

Goal 2: Give "Marriage Insurance" to the Engaged

By training couples with healthy marriages to be Mentor Couples, who administer the inventory and review communication-building exercises, ministers can give couples a 95 percent chance their marriage will go the distance. Such couple-to-couple mentoring was unknown when Harriet and I began it in 1992.

Mentoring doubles the percentage of engaged couples who decide not to marry to one fifth, thus preventing more weak marriages and divorces.

Goal 3: Enrich All Existing Marriages

Churches conduct an annual enrichment event featuring a marital inventory, speakers, or videos. For example, more than a thousand couples in Sioux Falls have attended a ten-part DVD series *(10 Great Dates to Energize Your Marriage,*[2] by David and Claudia Arp) on consecutive Saturday nights. The congregation offers free babysitting, making participation easy. After watching twenty minutes of a DVD on such topics as "Resolving Honest Conflict," "Becoming an Encourager," or "Building a Creative Love Life," couples go to a restaurant for dessert and coffee, complete a brief exercise in the paperback study guide/workbook, *10 Great Dates* by David and Claudia Arp. The kit includes a *10 Great Dates* paperback and a Leader's Guide. This is an inexpensive way to breathe new life into any marriage.

Another way to offer marriage enrichment in one weekend is to use the REFOCCUS marital inventory. One inventory category is covered Friday night, two Saturday morning, and two more in the afternoon. REFOCCUS is a proven and effective resource for couples to determine where their relationship is strong and what issues need attention. It assesses relational strengths so couples can address challenges with confidence and hope. It also helps them to reflect on their marriage and to talk about the growth and change each spouse has experienced. Corresponding couple exercises deepen discussion. Scripture readings set a religious tone, and couple leaders provide positive role models as they share triumphs and struggles from their own marriage, giving participants "permission" to be open and honest with each other.

A REFOCCUS weekend offers couples a place, a time, and a structured and positive environment to reflect on their marriage and learn how to be intentional about future growth. The *REFOCCUS Manual for Extended Use* makes it easy for a pastor or group of couples to organize and conduct such a weekend.[3]

Goal 4: Restore Troubled Marriages

Using trained "back-from-the-brink couples" to mentor other couples in crisis can help save four out of five troubled marriages. *Consumer*

Testimonials about REFOCCUS Weekends

- "It was a great way to reconnect with your spouse. It promotes heartfelt communication."
- "Things we usually don't talk about were more comfortable to discuss."
- "It helped us discuss all of our unknown issues. And it gave us ways to explain and hear without having to nag each other."
- "It helped us open up and highlight areas needing attention."

Reports asked couples in troubled marriages whether they were helped by professional counselors: only 16 percent responded affirmatively, and not all of those marriages were saved. By contrast, in 1990 Father Richard McGinnis and his wife, Phyllis, created Marriage Ministry, a group of seven trained couples in Jacksonville, Florida, who, in five years saved thirty-eight out of forty marriages headed for divorce.[4] That's a 95 percent success rate—a stark contrast to the disappointing results of professional therapists.[5]

Consider the following cases from McGinnis's church:

- One husband had such a severe drinking problem he lost his job and was out of work for two years.
- A wife was involved in adultery for eight years.
- Another husband was bisexual and had homosexual affairs early in his marriage; his wife was in and out of a mental institution three times.

- A prosthodontist was trying to pay off his $200,000 dental-school debt by doing his own lab work at night, prompting his wife to lament, "What kind of marriage is this? I never see you."

Each couple's marriage survived. Father McGinnis helped them to transform their past misery into ministry. Marriage Ministry gives couples in marital distress hope and help to heal their marriages. Recovered couples, once on the brink of divorce, struggling with issues of adultery, addiction, abuse, and so on, can be equipped to serve as "marriage menders" to assist other couples facing similar challenges. Past pain can serve God's purpose.

Goal 5: Reconcile Separated Couples

Our culture views separation as a prelude to divorce; but separation can become a time for personal growth for the spouse trying to save the marriage. Joe and Michelle Williams each had three failed marriages before they married each other, but their fourth marriage has endured for more than twenty years. From their experiences, they created a self-guided workbook course, *Reconciling God's Way*.[6] Their program is designed to help couples when one spouse wants to save the marriage but the other wants out.

The abandoned spouse does the exercises in the workbook and asks a same-gender friend to meet with him or her one hour a week for twelve weeks. The friend is given a *Support Partner Handbook* to assist in the important role of "accountability partner." The spouse reads a chapter of Proverbs every day to gain a biblical perspective on his or her role in the failure of the marriage. According to its authors, the course heals more than half of separated couples' marriages and 75 percent of marriages when spouses are living under the same roof.[7]

Goal 6: Help Stepfamilies Succeed

Stepfamily Support Groups give couples with children from a previous marriage or relationship a place and a plan to learn how to be successful parents and partners. This is particularly important for cohabiting couples who marry. Without help, 70 percent will divorce,[8] often for a second or third time, traumatizing their children yet again. In 2005 two million cohabiting couples had children under eighteen living with them—that's 41 percent of all cohabiting couples. Half of those couples had previous marriages, and another third of cohabiting couples had kids from previous unwed relationships. If churches create Stepfamily Support Groups, 80 percent of those couples can be successful.

Stepparents come to support groups to learn from more experienced stepparents how to address issues that are unique to blended families. Though Harriet and I are in a primary marriage, we started a ministry at our church called Stepfamilies Offering Support. How? We followed detailed advice on how to do so in Rev. Dick Dunn's manual *Creating a Successful Stepfamily Ministry.*[9]

DO COMMUNITY MARRIAGE POLICIES WORK?

First Things First, of Chattanooga, Tennessee, organized local clergy to adopt a Community Marriage Policy in 1997. Over the years about 150 more churches have signed on, and others are cooperating. An engaged couple, unaware of the Community Marriage Policy, asked their pastor at Signal Mountain Presbyterian Church to marry them within a month. He replied:

> We don't do it that quickly here. We need time to administer a premarital inventory, a detailed questionnaire that

will give you an assessment of your relationship strengths and growth areas. A trained Mentor Couple will be assigned to you to facilitate discussion of inventory responses. Six mentoring sessions of two to two and a half hours are scheduled biweekly over three to four months. Mentors will also teach you skills to improve your communication and ability to resolve conflict. We also have a series of lectures on the biblical perspective of marriage.

Finally, I must add that 10 to 20 percent of couples who go through this program decide not to marry. And studies show that those who break up after taking an inventory have the same scores as those who marry and later divorce. So those couples are avoiding a bad marriage before it has even begun. However, I also can say that virtually all of the couples who do marry are able to build a marriage that goes the distance. We call it "marriage insurance!"

As the couple left the church, the young man said to his fiancée, "We don't need this. We love each other; we love the Lord. Why should we jump through all these hoops?" They got in their car, drove down from Signal Mountain, and stopped at a Baptist church, repeating their request: "We'd like to be married here next month."

The Baptist pastor said, "Why?" Somewhat surprised, the young man stammered, "You have a beautiful church."

"I'm sorry, I don't believe I recognize you. Are you Baptists? What church do you attend?"

"Signal Mountain Presbyterian," they acknowledged.

"Why aren't you getting married there?"

"Well, our pastor has all these requirements for couples marrying there—Mentor Couples, taking an inventory and classes. He said it would take a minimum of four months."

"Oh, we have the same requirements here," the Baptist pastor replied. "In fact, you won't find a church in Chattanooga that will marry you in a month. Nearly 150 churches here have signed a Community Marriage Policy in which clergy pledged to require four months of marriage preparation. The city's divorce rate has fallen more than 20 percent as a result. You might as well go back to your own church."

They did.

In most communities, couples like this are in charge of when they marry. Pastors will accede to their demands to marry in a short time. Yet often the couples have no idea how to make a marriage work. Typically, they've never heard of a premarital inventory or a Mentor Couple and don't know the value of either.

All churches in a community should have a shared knowledge of how to help couples successfully bond for a lifetime. Unfortunately, most congregations operate independently rather than interdependently.

The *Yearbook of American and Canadian Churches 2007* lists three hundred denominations, and the United States is a nation of tens of thousands of independent churches unaffiliated with any denomination.[10] In fact, America has more than 300,000 Protestant churches (and nearly 20,000 Catholic churches). Typically, local Protestant churches perceive themselves as being in competition with each other for members.[11] That's why most Protestant clergy will agree to marry a couple in a month: a pastor rationalizes that if he marries them, they might become members of his church. Couples can play one pastor against another to find one with the least requirements. The result is that most communities have no marriage standards.

In a Community Marriage Policy, pastors set aside denominational differences and agree on minimum standards for marriage preparation. In a typical city, the reforms for thorough marriage preparation have been agreed upon by forty to sixty pastors across denominational lines. In Austin, Texas, 252 pastors and priests signed on; in the Twin

Cities of Minneapolis–St. Paul, 300 ministers signed covenants to adopt the reforms described here.

Dropping Divorce Rates

A number of cities reported that their divorce rates fell after they signed a Community Marriage Policy. For example, Peoria, Illinois, signed its CMP in September 1991. In that year they had 1,210 divorces. The very next year, 1992, they had only 947 divorces, and the number remained below 1,000 throughout the 1990s—a lasting one-fifth drop in the divorce rate.

Skeptics asked, "What about the other hundred-plus cities that signed on?" They noted, "The U.S. divorce rate is dropping. Are you taking credit for what is already happening?"

The National Fatherhood Institute obtained a Justice Department grant to fund the Institute for Research and Evaluation to evaluate the impact of Community Marriage Policies. Researchers Paul James Birch, Stan E. Weed, and Joseph Olsen examined the first 114 CMPs in 122 counties signed by the year 2000. Their study, "Assessing the Impact of Community Marriage Policies on County Divorce Rates," was published in the journal *Family Relations*.[12]

To control for the slightly dropping divorce rate, they took into account two sets of information:

1. *Pre- and post-comparisons*—The institute compared the decline of divorces in CMP cities/counties for five years before the CMP was implemented with the divorce rate seven years after CMP implementation. It found the divorce decline in CMP counties "accelerated" to fall "almost twice as fast" as before clergy had signed the CMP. Divorce rates declined by 1.4 percent per year before the CMP adoption and by 2.3 percent a year afterward.

2. *CMP counties vs. comparison counties*—The Institute for Research and Evaluation then compared the results of CMP counties with counties in each state where the divorce-rate decline was virtually the same before the CMP but that did not sign a CMP covenant. This was a difficult, complex task. Researchers had to examine the divorce rates of all three thousand counties in America to select those in each state whose divorce rates in the pre-CMP period most closely resembled the CMP county experience before clergy agreed to the covenant. The Institute found that CMP counties enjoyed a 2 percent greater decline in divorce per year than did comparison counties.

If stretched out over seven years, CMP counties reflected a 17.5 percent drop in the divorce rate—nearly double the 9.4 percent decline in control counties. When these results were announced at the National Press Club in April 2004, Dr. Stan Weed, the institute's president, commented:

> The results reported are important, not because of their magnitude, which is modest, but because there are any results at all. The deck was stacked against finding a program effect.
>
> Community Marriage Policies depend on local volunteers of varying degrees of motivation, commitment and ability and with high turnover. There's wide variation in program implementation. The proportion of signed congregations is often small, while the data is county-wide. Serious training of mentor couples began in 1998. Under these conditions, finding a significant program effect is actually pretty surprising.

One reporter asked, "How many marriages were saved by Community Marriage Policies?" Weed estimated that in the 122 counties,

"About thirty-one thousand divorces were averted and that is a conservative estimate. It is not at all unreasonable to say there were fifty thousand, through the year 2001."

By 2007, with six more years of progress in the initial cities and 106 new CMPs in place, perhaps 100,000 couples have avoided divorce as a result of Community Marriage Policies.

This is evidence that *if* clergy cooperate across denominational lines in their local community, with a conscious plan to reduce the divorce rate, they *are* able to do so.

Diane Sollee, director of Smart Marriages and the former associate director of the American Association for Marriage and Family Therapy, noted in her remarks at the National Press Club: "I come out of what I call the therapy industry. As therapy grew in power and acceptance in 1960s, 70s, and 80s, we took marriage away from congregations and the community. Sophisticated clergy persons knew that if a couple is having trouble, they should refer them out to the experts. This research and this Community Marriage Policy program with Marriage Savers churches shows how important it is to put marriages back into the churches and the communities who can take better care of them."

Curtailing Cohabitation Rates

What's particularly relevant for this book is that the Institute for Research and Evaluation's study also revealed a striking decline in cohabitation rates from 1990 to 2000 in CMP communities, while cohabitation rates rose substantially in comparison counties where clergy did not adopt a CMP. Cohabitation rates *fell* by 13.4 percent in cities with Community Marriage Policies; they *rose* by 19.2 percent in comparison counties. Thus, by the end of the 1990s, CMP counties enjoyed one-third lower cohabitation rates than carefully matched counties (13.4 percent plus 19.2 equals 32.6 percent). This was a welcome but unanticipated result.

Why was it unexpected? Historically, Marriage Savers has focused on saving marriages—not on persuading cohabiting couples to form healthy unions and marry. Other than one small pilot project, we have concentrated on helping couples prepare for, enrich, and restore traditional marriages.

Another reason we were surprised that CMP cities had reduced cohabitation rates for the decade of 1990 to 2000 is that in 1990 only ten cities and counties had a Community Marriage Policy. By 1995, at mid-decade, there were just 26 CMP communities. The rest of the 114 CMPs in the study were signed in the latter half of the decade. Chattanooga and Minneapolis–St. Paul signed in 1997. That left only the years 1998 and 1999 to have an impact on the cohabitation rate for the entire decade.

Yet the impact was not only measurable but substantial; one-third lower cohabitation rates in CMP cities than in the control cities.

Marriage Savers is the only organization that has reduced divorce and cohabitation rates in more than one hundred cities.

HOW DO WE START A COMMUNITY MARRIAGE POLICY IN OUR CITY?

America boasts nearly 350,000 churches, synagogues, and mosques. While 10,000 houses of worship have signed a CMP pledging to implement marital reforms, that's a small percentage of the total.

However, about 800,000 couples a year take a premarital inventory. That's a substantial number. So we suggest that clergy who already use a premarital inventory take the next step and train a core of Mentor Couples to take over that task. It will lighten the pastor's workload while tapping the wisdom and time of couples with healthy marriages to coach the next generation of couples. While mentors are a supplement to, not a substitute for, a pastor, a couple who is in their fifties and no longer has children at home likely has time to invest in another couple that a pastor does not. A married man and woman can model and discuss how to make marriage work. It's easy for mentors to facilitate discussion of relational issues such as managing finances, addressing in-law problems, resolving conflict, and sharing parenting styles.

Currently, few churches use trained Mentor Couples as part of marriage preparation. Yet every church has couples who could participate in such a ministry. Because one Mentor Couple can handle only two couples per year at most, it is necessary to train a number of couples. A church with twenty weddings a year ideally would have fifteen Mentor Couples. Understandably, some mentors will inevitably be unable to participate from time to time, due to other obligations.

Couples who cohabit—who make up the majority of those now planning to marry—especially need rigorous marriage preparation. Their experience has taught them wrong lessons about relationships. However, as the case study of our mentoring Hector and Teresa demonstrates, even highly conflicted cohabiting couples can be helped to form successful marriages with the assistance of mature, healthy Mentor Couples that can be recruited and trained in any congregation.

HOW CAN WE MAKE OUR CMP LAUNCHING A BIG EVENT?

When Marriage Savers helps clergy plan the signing of a Community Marriage Policy, we urge that it be made a major event, one the press would like to cover. As a journalist, I write a press release that helps spark coverage by both local and regional newspapers, plus local television stations. First, I provide data on the county's declining marriage rate and its often surprisingly high divorce rate.[13] I emphasize that never before has that community's pastors and priests bonded together, across denominational lines, to set marriage standards with the goal of reducing the divorce rate. I also summarize the track record of Community Marriage Policies in reducing both divorce and cohabitation rates. Personal calls to reporters are also made in advance to secure coverage.

At our suggestion, clergy gather on the steps of the local courthouse at 1:00 p.m. on a Friday. After brief remarks by Harriet and me, by the clergy organizer, and perhaps by the mayor and a judge, pastors line up to sign an enlarged version of the covenant. After signing, pastors walk to the microphone to say, in a sentence or two, why they're taking this step. The event makes a great news story for local newspapers and television. As a newsman since 1961, my goal is to get the story on page one of the newspaper and on the evening TV news. When we were in state capitals, such as Madison, Wisconsin, and Cheyenne, Wyoming, clergy signed the CMP under the dome of the capitol. The governor of Wyoming personally congratulated the clergy for taking steps to reduce the divorce rate—which would save taxpayers millions of dollars. In both state capitals, the story was covered by every local television station and made a statewide news story.

Even when the signing is held in a small town, what participating ministers say is often eloquent and easily quotable by the media. In our remarks at such signings, Harriet says, "This is a historic day. You will look back upon this day as a new day for marriage in this community, and an old day for divorce."

I add:

> Behind us is a courthouse where they give out marriage licenses on one side of the building and divorce decrees on the other. We predict you will see an increase in business on the marriage side and a decrease on the divorce side. In Modesto, California, the first city where clergy signed a Community Marriage Policy, in 1986, the di-

vorce rate has *plunged to half what it was, and the number of marriages has nearly doubled*—from 1,300 a year to 2,500. Furthermore, an independent study reports that cohabitation rates are down by a third in more than one hundred cities. This is a total reversal of national trends.

I then outline the five reforms we will train clergy and Mentor Couples to implement: helping couples prepare for a lifelong marriage; enriching existing marriages; restoring troubled marriages; reconciling separated couples; and helping stepfamilies to be successful.

Press coverage of a Community Marriage Policy signing sends three important messages:

1. *Marriage matters—not just to individuals but to the whole society.* The event provides a way for clergy to publicly communicate, as a united front, that marriage is central to the well-being of the family and that they are committed to making marriage a priority in their congregations.
2. *The church has a sacred responsibility to take the lead in building healthy marriages.* While the church has not always done so in the past, area clergy are now assuming the role of promoting, preserving, and protecting the institution of marriage. In fact, by making the signing a public event, organizers know more ministers will participate.
3. *Cohabitation is a counterfeit of marriage, a shabby substitute that is best avoided.* Religious leaders articulate that there is a better way to test a relationship than by living together. The evidence is in the reversal of soaring cohabitation rates.

A Community Marriage Policy nudges more churches to provide a biblical and practical alternative to cohabitation. Thorough marriage preparation in our home church resulted in a remarkably low 3 percent failure rate over a decade. Compare that with the 80-plus percent failure rate of cohabitation before or after unprepared marriage. With more churches awakening to the need to address this daunting issue, more and more pre-marital couples will be helped to take the wiser course.

A Community Marriage Policy gives church leaders an opportunity to take a public stand for marriage as God's first institution, the foundation of a civilized society, the bedrock of the family. Evangelical and mainline Protestants join Catholic priests affirming the centrality of marriage. Dr. Robert Smith, the pastor who organized the Alamagordo, New Mexico, Community Marriage Policy, asserted: "I think it's one of the best things that I have ever known in my ministry . . . and it has such a wonderful potential for changing communities. I think it's precisely the kind of thing [the apostle] Paul would be promoting!"

NEW FEDERAL FUNDING FOR "HEALTHY MARRIAGE INITIATIVES"

On February 8, 2006, President George W. Bush signed welfare reauthorization that included, for the first time, a funding stream of a hundred million dollars per year for five years to promote marriage. The first round of applications were made in June 2006 and funded in September. On the day the law was signed, Dr. Wade Horn, then assistant secretary of the U.S. Department of Health and Human Services, who had crafted and fought for the measure, participated in a Family Research Council panel, "Saving Marriages One Community at a Time," to honor Marriage Savers for the signing by clergy of the 200th Community Marriage Policy in Las Cruces, New Mexico. Dr. Horn, one of the original Marriage Savers board members, referred to part of the law to create a "Community Healthy Marriage Initiative," which he said is kind of modeled after your Community Marriage Policy. It asks what it would look like if we, as a community, were serious about supporting couples in forming and sustaining healthy marriages? It would be providing relationship education to young people, greater access for marriage premarital education, education for the already married, greater access to marital outreach in troubled marriages.

If that sounds a lot like the work of Marriage Savers, that is no accident. In fact, I am here today to tell you that to a very large extent—the $100 million in the President's Healthy Marriage Initiative would not be where it is today and would not be structured as it is, if it were not for the work of the McManuses. They started with a dream, a vision that churches need to do more to prepare couples for marriage, more to help couples sustain a healthy marriage, and reach out to troubled couples. It is a great delight to draw attention to your work and pay tribute to it.[14]

A CALL TO ACTION

Modern culture has lulled millions of people into irresponsible intimacy without moral obligations. Almost without notice, the nation has witnessed a twelvefold increase in cohabitation, which has sparked a disastrous drop in the marriage rate, a huge increase in babies born out of wedlock, and a persistently high divorce rate. The rampant increase in living together as an alternate but acceptable form of family life has profoundly contributed to the declining significance of the institution of marriage in America—and in most Western societies.

The church, as society's guardian of values, can no longer tolerate our culture's casual attitude toward "relationships without strings and marriages without rings," as David Popenoe has put it. The numbers soundly document the harm of cohabitation to individuals, their relationships, and their children. If we are to assure our children and our children's children of a bright future, the church must speak out and take action to implement known strategies to prevent further family disintegration and to increase family stability.

The notion that living together is a trial marriage is a myth.

The "conventional wisdom" that cohabitation is harmless—just another form of dating—is a lie, and it's putting millions of people at risk.

Marriage—and the church's active support of it—is the answer.

Sample of a Community Marriage Policy

Hardin County, Elizabethtown, Kentucky

WHY A MARRIAGE COVENANT?

What type of positive change in American family life could improve the overall well being of married couples and children in Hardin County? Many believe that the answer comes by strengthening the marriage relationship and increasing the probability of children being born and raised in healthy, married, two-parent homes with a father and mother both providing guidance and nurture.

Some hold this view because of their spiritual belief that marriage, between a man and a woman, and the family are institutions ordained by God. Others base their support on evidence that children of such families have significantly lower rates of poverty, teenage pregnancy, school dropout, delinquency, and substance abuse.

With 75 percent of all marriages taking place in houses of worship, the clergy can play a critical role in laying a foundation for a lifelong partnership.

Our secular community, likewise has a role to play by reviewing its organizations and businesses and finding ways in which it can strengthen marital relationships and family life.

Definition

A Community Marriage Covenant is a set of agreed-upon guidelines for premarital preparation and community support for marriages. Its purpose is to empower couples for healthy, lifelong marriage and to raise the standard of two-parent families within the community.

This community covenant is not intended to imply criticism of single-parent families, nor does it assume that abusive situations should be endured.

The Current Trends—A Cause for Concern

- In the last five full calendar years (2002–2006) a total of 4,954 marriages have been filed in the Hardin County Clerk's office.
- In the same time the Administrative Office of the Courts reports that during that period a total of 3,814 divorces were filed in the county.
- Those figures suggest that married couples need assistance in their marriages to ensure that problems are resolved and that marriages are strengthened.

HARDIN COUNTY MARRIAGE COVENANT

This covenant expresses the common concerns of the faith community regarding the need to strengthen proposed and existing marriages.

We Believe:

- God has established the sanctity and companionship of marriage in Scripture.

- God intends the marriage bond of husband and wife to be a lifelong union.
- As religious leaders, we have a responsibility to participate in and to provide premarital preparation to improve the understanding and mutual commitment of couples being married.
- As religious leaders, we have a responsibility to strengthen and nourish existing marriages.

Therefore we will:

- Encourage courtships of at least one year.
- Affirm abstinence outside marriage and fidelity within marriage.
- Provide mentoring for engaged couples that will utilize Scripture, a premarital inventory, and teaching of communication skills (a process lasting approximately four months).
- Offer two post-wedding mentoring sessions with clergy or mentors in the first year of marriage.
- Train mature married couples to be Mentoring Couples serving engaged and couples in crisis.
- Enrich all existing marriages with an annual retreat held at the church at low cost.
- Reconcile the separated with a workbook course, "Reconciling God's Way."
- Heal hurting marriages with couples whose own marriages nearly failed, to mentor crisis couples.
- Create Stepfamily Support Groups to help couples with stepchildren to be successful.
- Share resources with other congregations and community organizations to strengthen marriages.

RATIONALE

To Reduce the Rate of Divorce:

An important study released in 2004 stated that the first 114 communities with a Community Marriage Policy reduced their divorce rate by 17.5 percent over seven years, saving 50,000 marriages through 2001. With six more years and twice as many CMPs, perhaps 100,000 divorces were averted.

To Reduce the Rate of Cohabitation:

The same study reported that from 1990 to 2000, cities with a Community Marriage Covenant ended the decade with a cohabitation rate one-third lower than those without a CMC. By contrast, the number of cohabiting couples has soared twelvefold since 1960, from 430,000 to 5.2 million in 2005.

To Raise the Rate of Marriage:

Modesto, Calif., the first city to create a Community Marriage Policy, saw its number of marriages rise from 1,300 in 1986 to 2,500 in 2005. Evansville, Ind., reports a 16 percent rise in the marriage rate from 1998 to 2004–2005. This is in stark contrast with the 50 percent drop in the U.S. marriage rate from 1970 to 2005.

To Encourage Lengthy Courtships:

Short courtships before marriage—that is, courtships lasting less than a year—are associated with a higher risk of divorce.

To Expect a Premarital Process:

A Gallup Poll found that 57 percent of all marriages fail due to poor communication and conflict-resolution skills. In 38 percent of those divorces, couples say they were aware of those problems when they married or soon afterward.

To Initiate a Mentor Couples Program:

Trained mature married couples will serve as mentors to work with engaged couples, newlyweds, and those experiencing marital difficulties.

To Encourage Marriage-Enrichment Opportunities:

Nine out of ten couples attending marriage enrichment weekends, seminars, or classes believe that the experiences strengthened their marriages.

FREQUENTLY ASKED QUESTIONS

- **Why have a long courtship?** Courtships lasting less than a year are associated with a higher risk of divorce. A leisurely pace to courtship produces marriages that last.
- **What's wrong with cohabitation?** First, cohabitation has diverted millions from marrying. There were 21 million never-married Americans in 1970, but 52 million in 2005. Second, many people think of cohabitation as a "trial marriage." Instead it is a trial for divorce. Those who do marry after cohabiting are 50 percent more likely to divorce than those who do not

live together before marriage. And 75 percent of children born to cohabiting couples will experience separation of their parents before they reach sixteen years of age.

- **Why have premarital mentoring?** Of 288 couples mentored in one church during the 1990s, fifty-five couples decided *not* to marry. Studies show such couples avoided a bad marriage before it began. However, there were only 7 divorces of 233 couples who married over a decade. That's a divorce rate of only 3 percent. A 97 percent success rate over ten years is virtual "marriage insurance."
- **What is a Mentor Couple?** Mentor Couples have healthy marriages and can be found in any church. They have been trained to help other couples prepare for, enrich, or restore their marriages.
- **Why have post-wedding mentoring?** Nine out of ten couples participating in post-wedding sessions (mentoring opportunities, classes, seminars, or marriage enrichment weekends) report that the experience strengthened their marriages.
- **Does a Community Marriage Covenant really make a difference?** A 2004 study shows that the 114 communities that already have such a policy reported an average 17.5 percent drop in divorces in seven years.

This marriage covenant is a work in progress, and we invite and encourage other churches, organizations, and individuals to become involved with us in strengthening marriages in Hardin County.

If you wish to discuss the covenant or add your name to the growing list of supporters, please contact either Elizabethtown Ministerial Association or the Radcliff Ministerial Association.

220 Cities with Community Marriage Policies/Covenants

ON JUNE 22, 2007, twenty-four clergy signed the 220th Community Marriage Policy, in Cecil County, Maryland. After the signing, we asked Mentor Couples and clergy to implement the covenant from 6:30 to 10:00 on Friday evening and 8:30 a.m. to 5:00 p.m. on Saturday. The goal of the training is to put a safety net under every marriage, virtually eliminating divorce in participating churches.

U.S. Cities

ALABAMA
Huntsville
Montgomery
Opelika
Tuscaloosa

ALASKA
Fairbanks
Kenai Peninsula
Wassilla

ARIZONA
Yuma

ARKANSAS
Hot Springs
Mena
Russellville
Springdale

CALIFORNIA
Atwater
Bakersfield
Davis
Fresno
Modesto
Riverside
Sacramento
Santa Barbara
Tracy
Turlock
Vacaville
Vallejo
Ventura

COLORADO
Colorado Springs
Denver
Montrose

CONNECTICUT
Bethel
Fairfield
New Fairfield

DELAWARE
Dover

FLORIDA
Clearwater
Homestead
Jacksonville
Lake Wales
Lutz
Melbourne
Naples
Palatka
Sarasota
Tallahassee

GEORGIA
Albany
Columbus
Dalton
Rome

IDAHO
Nampa

ILLINOIS
Auburn
Aurora
Moline/Rock Island
Morris
Peoria
Quincy
Rockford
Waukegan

INDIANA
Bloomington
Boomville
Crawfordsville
Dyer
Evansville
Hamilton City
Kokomo
Mount Vernon
Muncie
New Castle
New Hartford
Porter County
Princeton

IOWA
Bettendorf
Cedar Rapids
Clear Lake
Davenport
Sioux City

KANSAS
Bonner Springs
Kansas City
Lawrence
Lenexa/Overland Park
Manhattan
Salina
Shawnee

KENTUCKY
Elizabethtown
Lexington
Louisville
Owensboro
Pineville
Stanford

LOUISIANA
Alexandria
Baton Rouge
Minden
Ruston
Shreveport

MAINE
Portland

MARYLAND
Burtonsville
Cecil County
Frederick
Westminster

MICHIGAN
Adrian
Coldwater
Grand Rapids
Harbor Springs
Lansing
Port Huron
Rockford

Sturgis
Traverse City

MINNESOTA
Mankato
Minneapolis–St. Paul
Pipestone

MISSISSIPPI
Jackson

MISSOURI
Cape Giradeau
Kansas City
Springfield

NEBRASKA
Chaldron
Fremont
Kearney
Lexington
Omaha

NEW HAMPSHIRE
Amherst-Milton
Raymond

NEW JERSEY
Flemington
Toms River
Whippany

NEW MEXICO
Alamogordo
Farmington
Las Cruces

NEW YORK
Albany
Canandaigua
Jamestown

NORTH CAROLINA
Cary
Greensboro
Hickory
Wilmington
Winston-Salem

NORTH DAKOTA
Grand Forks

OHIO
Canton
Cleveland
Cuyahoga Falls
Fremont
Galion
London
Millersburg
Springfield
Urbana
Xenia
Zanesville

OKLAHOMA
Stillwater
Tulsa

OREGON
Brownsville
Clackamas
Corvallis
Grants Pass
Junction City
Lebanon
McMinniville
Milton-Freewater
Philomath
Salem-Kaiser
Sweet Home

PENNSYLVANIA
Beaver
Boyerton
Erie
Hershey
Manheim
New Holland
Reading

SOUTH CAROLINA
Aiken
Greenville
Sumter

SOUTH DAKOTA
Mitchell
Sioux Falls

TENNESSEE
Chattanooga
Cleveland
Dyersburg
Franklin
Memphis
Nashville

TEXAS
Abilene
Austin
Brazos Point
Dallas
El Paso
Flower Mound
Forney
McKinney
Paris
Tyler
Waxahachie

VIRGINIA
Culpeper
Harrisonburg
Leesburg
Lynchburg
Newport News

Richmond
Woodbridge

WASHINGTON
Auburn
Bellingham
Ellensburg
Pasco
Richland
Southwest Seattle
Spokane
Tacoma

WEST VIRGINIA
Charleston
Martinsburg

WISCONSIN
Burlington
Eau Claire
Elkhorn
Fond du Lac
Fox Valley
Madison
New Holstein
Tomah
Wausau
Wisconsin Rapids

WYOMING
Cheyenne

Foreign Cities

BAHAMAS

Nassau

CANADA

Cloverdale, British Columbia

ENGLAND

Bath
Bristol
York

Notes

Chapter 1: A Beach Encounter

1. Mary Howitt, "The Spider and the Fly," in *Bartlett's Familiar Quotations* 15th ed., Emily Morison Beck, ed. (Boston: Little, Brown and Co., 1980).

Chapter 2: Why Couples Live Together

1. Cohabiting.org doesn't present its data as a scientific survey but rather as the results of readers who completed the questionnaire, 75 percent of whom were women.

2. Andrew Cherlin, "The Deinstitutionalization of American Marriage," *Journal of Marriage and Family* 66 (November 2004): 849.

3. Cohabiting.org, "Cohabiting Couples Survey," http://members.aol.com/Cohabiting/survey.htm, accessed July 2007.

4. Ibid.

5. Judith Wallerstein, Julia Lewis, and Sandra Blakeslee, *The Unexpected Legacy of Divorce: A 25-Year Landmark Study* (New York: Hyperion, 2000), 31.

6. Cohabiting.org, "Cohabiting Couples Survey."

7. Chapter 9 tells the detailed story of our mentoring Teresa and Hector.

8. Wallerstein, Lewis, and Blakeslee, *The Unexpected Legacy of Divorce.*

9. Larry Bumpass and Hsien-Hen Lu, "Trends in Cohabitation and Implications for Children's Family Contexts in the United States," *Population Studies* 54, no. 1 (March 2000): 28–41.

10. Bumpass, 1998. Quoted in Wendy Manning and Pamela Smock, "Measuring and Modeling Cohabitation: New Perspectives from Qualitative Data," *Journal of Marriage and Family* 67 (November 2005): 989.

11. Barbara Dafoe Whitehead and David Popenoe, "Why Men Won't Commit: Exploring Young Men's Attitudes about Sex, Dating and Marriage," *The State of Our Unions: The Social Health of Marriage in America, 2002* (The National Marriage Project).

12. Cohabiting.org, "Testimonials Taken Unedited from the Guestbook," http://members.aol.com/cohabiting/test.htm, accessed July 2007.

13. Whitehead and Popenoe, "Why Men Won't Commit," 6–7.

14. Ibid.

15. Ibid., 11.

16. Scott M. Stanley, *The Power of Commitment: A Guide to Active, Lifelong Love* (San Francisco: Jossey-Bass, 2005), 152.

17. David Gudgel, *Before You Live Together* (Ventura, Calif.: Regal Books, 2003), 34.

18. Jeff Van Goethem, *Living Together: A Guide to Counseling Unmarried Couples* (Grand Rapids, Mich.: Kregel, 2005), 47.

19. Stanley, *Power of Commitment,* 156–57.

20. Nancy Wartik, "The Perils of Playing House," *Psychology Today* (July/August 2005): 46.

21. Dorian Solot, "Seniors Living Happily in Sin," *The Early Show,* CBS, August 26, 2002.

22. Alex Roberts and David Blankenhorn, "The Other Marriage Penalty: A New Proposal to Eliminate the Marriage Penalty for Low-Income Americans," Research Brief No. 3, November 2006 (Institute for American Values).

23. Senator Sam Brownback (R-Kans.) in a press conference, May 2007.

CHAPTER 3: RISKS OF COHABITATION

1. Judith Krantz, quoted in *Marriage Savers: Helping Your Friends and Family Avoid Divorce,* rev. ed., Michael J. McManus (Grand Rapids, Mich.: Zondervan, 1993, 1995), 40.

2. Cohabiting.org, "Cohabiting Facts," http://members.aol.com/cohabiting/facts.htm, accessed July 2007.

3. Gudgel, *Before You Live Together,* 53.

4. Ibid., 53–54.

5. K. C. Scott, "Mom, I Want to Live with My Boyfriend," *Reader's Digest,* February 1994, 77.

6. "Relationship Quality Differs Little for Cohabitors and Marrieds," *Penn State University News,* February 20, 1997, http://www.psu.edu/ur/NEWS/news/cohabitation.html.

7. Cohabiting.org, "Archived Message Board," http://members.aol .com/cohabiting/message2.htm. Minor corrections made for readability.

8. Jan E. Stets, "Cohabiting and Marital Aggression: The Role of Social Isolation"*Journal of Marriage and the Family,* 53 (1991): 669–80.

9. Ibid., 674.

10. Linda J. Waite and Maggie Gallagher, *The Case for Marriage: Why Married People Are Happier, Healthier, and Better Off Financially* (New York: Doubleday, 2000), 155.

11. Kersti Yllo and Murray A. Straus, "Interpersonal Violence Among Married and Cohabiting Couples," *Family Relations* (1981): 30.

12. Callie Marie Rennison, "Intimate Partner Violence and Age of Victim, 1993–1999," Bureau of Justice Statistics Special Report, October 2001.

13. "America's Families and Living Arrangements," U.S. Census Report, 2003, 17.

14. Larry Bumpass, James Sweet, and Andrew Cherlin, "The Role of Cohabitation in Declining Rates of Marriage," *Journal of Marriage and the Family* 53 (November 1991): 913–27.

15. "Marital Status and Living Arrangement," U.S. Census, 2005.

16. Robert E. Rector, Kirk A. Johnson, Ph.D., Patrick F. Fagan, and Lauren R. Noyes, "Increasing Marriage Would Dramatically Reduce Child Poverty," Heritage Foundation, http://www.heritage.org/research/family/cda0306.cfm, accessed May 20, 2003.

17. " 'His' and 'Her' Marriage Expectations: Determinants and Consequences," *Fragile Families Research Brief* 23 (May 2004).

18. In 2004, 68.7 percent of all black births and 30.5 percent of white births were out of wedlock, according to the *National Vital Statistics Report* 50, 5.

19. "Statistical Abstracts" (1982, 1990, and 2003), U.S. Census Bureau and National Center for Health Statistics, 2006.

20. Pat Fagan and Robert Rector, "The Effects of Divorce on America," Heritage Foundation Backgrounder, 2000.

21. Wendy D. Manning and Kathleen Lamb, "Parental Cohabitation and Adolescent Well-Being," Center for Family and Demographic Research, Bowling Green State University. An earlier draft was presented at the August 2000 meeting of the American Sociological Association in Anaheim, Calif.

22. R. Clark and S. Nelson, "Beyond the Two-Parent Family," paper presented at the annual meeting of the Population Association of America, March 23–25, 2000, Los Angeles, Calif.

23. Analysis by Peter Francese using Census Bureau Current Population Survey data, reported in *Washington Post,* March 4, 2007.

24. Edward O. Lauman et al., *The Social Organization of Sexuality: Sexual Practices in the United States,* (Chicago: University of Chicago Press, 1994).

25. Waite and Gallagher, *The Case for Marriage.*

26. Alfred DeMaris and Gerald R. Leslie, "Cohabitation with the Future Spouse: Its Influence upon Marital Satisfaction and Communication," *Journal of Marriage and the Family* 46 (February 1984): 77–84.

27. Dr. Laura Schlessinger, *Ten Stupid Things Women Do to Mess Up Their Lives* (New York: Villard Books, 1994).

28. Linda J. Ravdin, "Validity of Domestic Partnership Agreements in the Metro Area," in *The Pasternak & Fidis Reporter,* a publication of that Bethesda, Maryland, law firm, February 2005.

29. Ibid.

30. Cohabiting.org, "Legal Reasons," http://members.aol.com/cohabiting/legal.htm.

31. Joseph S. Lyles, *How You Can Avoid Legal Land Mines: A Layman's Guide to the Law* (Greenville, S.C.: R. J. Communications, 2002, 2003).

32. Cohabiting.org, "Archived Message Board," http://members.aol.com/cohabiting/message2.htm. Minor corrections made for readability.

33. Ibid.

34. Judith Krantz, quoted in *Marriage Savers,* p. 222.

Chapter 4: The Unpleasant Truth About Cohabitation

1. Jeffrey M. Jones, "Public Divided on Benefits of Living Together Before Marriage," The Gallup Organization, August 16, 2002.

2. Vigen Guroian, "Dorm Brothel," *Christianity Today,* February 2005.

3. Waite and Gallagher, *The Case for Marriage.*

4. Cohabiting.org, "The Problem of Cohabitation," http://members.aol.com/cohabiting/intro.htm.

5. "Recent Trends in Vital Statistics," *The World Almanac and Book of Facts 2007* (New York: World Almanac Books, 2007).

6. Bumpass and Lu, "Trends."

7. This is an estimate by the U.S. Census Bureau, which includes 4,855,000 couples who acknowledge they are living together and additional heterosexual couples who do not admit it but who are sharing the same household. Some are sexually inactive roommates. U.S. Bureau of the Census, Current Population Reports, Series P20–537; America's Families and Living Arrangements: March 2000; and U.S. Census, Population Division, Current Population Survey, 2005 Annual Social and Economic Supplement.

8. Whitehead and Popenoe, "Why Men Won't Commit."

9. "America's Families and Living Arrangements," U.S. Census Report, 2003.

10. Bumpass and Lu, "Trends," 29–41.

11. Pamela J. Smock and Wendy D. Manning, "Living Together Unmarried in the United States: Demographic Perspectives and Implications for Family Policy," *Law & Policy* 26, no. 1 (January 2004).

12. Cohabiting.org, "Archived Surveys: Cohabiting Couples and General Visitors."

13. R. R. Rindfuss and A. Vandenheuvel, "Cohabitation: A Precursor to Marriage or an Alternative to Being Single?" in *The Changing American*

Family: Sociological and Demographic Perspectives (Boulder, Colo.: Westview, 1992).

14. Robert Bernstein, U.S. Census interview, January 18, 2007.

15. Bumpass, Sweet, and Cherlin, "The Role of Cohabitation."

16. "Public Divided on Benefits of Living Together Before Marriage," Gallup Poll, August 16, 2002.

17. Bumpass, Sweet, and Cherlin, "The Role of Cohabitation," 913–27.

18. E. Mavis Hetherington in phone interview by Mike McManus, September 2006.

19. Lynda Lyons, "How Many Teens Are Cool with Cohabitation?" Gallup Poll, April 13, 2004.

20. Pamela Smock, "Living Together: Facts, Myths, about 'Living in Sin' Studied" (speech, University of Michigan Institute for Social Research, February 4, 2000).

21. Pamela Smock, "Cohabitation in the United States: An Appraisal of Research Themes, Findings, and Implications," *Annual Reviews Sociology* 26 (2000): 6.

22. Ibid., 7.

23. Paul Pearsall, Ph.D., *Ten Laws of Lasting Love* (New York: Simon & Schuster, 1993), 50.

24. Ibid., 50–51.

25. Ibid., 51.

26. Cohabiting.org, "The Problem of Cohabitation," *The State of Our Unions,* 2005.

CHAPTER 5: A CASE FOR MARRIAGE

1. "Public Divided on Benefits of Living Together Before Marriage," Gallup Poll, August 16, 2002, 3. More Americans give their marriages an A grade now (68 percent) than in 1996, when 59 percent did so.

2. David Olson, "Cohabiting Couples Have Lower Premarital Satisfaction," PREPARE/ENRICH newsletter, Fall 1988.

3. Cohabiting.org, "Archived Surveys: Cohabiting Couples and General Visitors."

4. Waite and Gallagher, *The Case for Marriage,* 67.

5. Ibid.

6. Ibid., 75.

7. Ibid.

8. Ibid., 148–49.

9. Ibid.

10. Linda J. Waite et al., "Does Divorce Make People Happy? Findings from a Study of Unhappy Marriages," Institute for American Values, 2002.

11. Susan Larson and David Larson, M.D., M.S.P.H., "Divorce: A Hazard to Your Health?" *Physician* (May/June 1990): 13.

12. James J. Lynch, *A Cry Unheard: New Insights into the Medical Consequences of Loneliness* (Baltimore, Md.: Bancroft Press, 2000), 97–105.

13. Waite and Gallagher, *The Case for Marriage,* 53.

14. Ibid.

15. Lynch, *A Cry Unheard,* 104.

16. Linda Waite's calculations from the Health and Retirement Survey.

17. Waite and Gallagher, *The Case for Marriage,* 48.

18. Bernard L. Cohen and I-Sing Lee, "A Catalogue of Risks," *Health Physics* 36 (1979): 707–22.

19. Waite and Gallagher, *The Case for Marriage,* 212 (footnote 14).

20. Ibid., 63–64.

21. Lynch, *A Cry Unheard,* 97.

22. Norval D. Glenn et al., "Why Marriage Matters: Twenty-one Conclusions from the Social Sciences," Institute for American Values, 2002, 10.

23. Waite and Gallagher, *The Case for Marriage,* 112.

24. Ibid., 113–14. Waite and Gallagher cite a paper presented to the Population Association of America by Lingxin Hao, "Family Structure, Private Transfers, and the Economic Well-Being of Families with Children."

25. "Current Population Survey," U.S. Census Bureau, March 2002.

26. Waite and Gallagher, *The Case for Marriage,* 79.

27. Ibid.

28. Ibid., 82.

29. Ibid., 82–83.

30. Ibid., 83.

31. S. M. Stanley, S. W. Whitton, and H. J. Markman, "Maybe I Do: Interpersonal Commitment and Premarital or Nonmarital Cohabitation," *Journal of Family Issues* 25 (2004): 496–519.

32. Waite and Gallagher, *The Case for Marriage,* 46.

CHAPTER 6: THE CHURCH'S RESPONSIBILITY

1. The Barna Group, "Born Again Adults Less Likely to Co-Habit, Just as Likely to Divorce," *The Barna Update,* August 6, 2001, http://www .barna.org/FlexPage.aspx?Page=BarnaUpdate&BarnaUpdateID=95.

2. In 2006 the Gallup Poll reported that 63 percent of Americans said they are "a member of a church or synagogue," and 40 percent attended services "in the last seven days."

3. Catholics note that Jesus strongly denounced divorce in the Gospels of Matthew, Mark, and Luke. When Pharisees asked, "Is it lawful for a man to divorce his wife?" (Mark 10:2), Jesus responded, "At the beginning of creation God 'made them male and female.' 'For this reason a man will leave his father and mother and be united to his wife, and the two will become one flesh.' So they are no longer two, but one. Therefore what God has joined together, let man not separate" (Mark 10:6–9). The disciples were stunned and asked him about it later, and Jesus added: "Anyone who divorces his wife and marries another woman commits adultery against her. And if she divorces her husband and marries another man, she commits adultery" (Mark 10:11–12). Matthew 19:9 contains an exception for "marital unfaithfulness" that is not found in Luke or Mark. However, adultery is not grounds for divorce in the Catholic Church. Catholics do grant fifty thousand annulments per year, after a marriage tribunal considers each case. That compares to two hundred thousand marriages a year, for a breakup rate of one in four, much less than the one in two U.S. average, which includes sixty-five million Catholics.

4. Catholic churches are so large—often ten to twenty times that of a typical Protestant church—that this is not an issue for them. In fact, Catholic

dioceses were the first to require a "Common Marriage Policy" with such standards as not scheduling a wedding for six to twelve months after the original appointment with a priest, requiring the taking of an inventory, and so on.

5. Peter D. Hart Research Associates, July 2003 poll.

6. Catherine Latimer and Michael J. McManus, "How to Give Marriage Insurance to Premarital Couples," http://www.marriagesavers.org/Marriage%20Insurance.htm, accessed August 2007.

7. Barbara Dafoe Whitehead and David Popenoe, *The State of Our Unions: The Social Health of Marriage in America* 2007 (The National Marriage Project).

8. See note 3 on U.S. church membership and attendance. For European data, Gallup published "Religion in Europe: Trust Not Filling the Pews." It reports that "weekly attendance at religious services is below 10% in France and Germany, 3% in Denmark, 5% in Finland and Sweden."

9. Data gathered by the Heritage Foundation in 2002 based on United Nations reports on ninety-two nations. Only Russia and Belarus, two former Soviet republics in economic chaos, have slightly higher divorce rates than the United States, plus the Maldives. When the U.S. rate was 4.1 per 1,000 people, it was 2.3 in Canada; 0.79 in China; 2.4 in Austria; 2.7 in Denmark; 1.2 in Egypt; 2.0 in France; 2.3 in Germany; 0.6 in Italy; 2.1 in South Korea; 1.1 in Poland; and 4.3 in Russia and Belarus.

10. The Barna Group, "Born-Again Christians Just as Likely to Divorce as Are Non-Christians," *The Barna Update,* September 8, 2004. How does this 35 percent divorce rate not contradict the 50 percent divorce rate often referred to? Since 1975 there has been one divorce for every two marriages; in that year there were 1.03 million divorces and 2.1 million marriages. That trend for three decades is the basis for saying that half of future marriages will end in divorce. However, some divorces are second or third divorces. So the actual percentage of *people* who have divorced is less than half.

11. Estimate is by Rev. Dick Dunn, who created the first Stepfamily Support Group at Roswell United Methodist Church.

12. Whitehead and Popenoe, "Why Men Won't Commit," 2.

Chapter 7: The Right Way to Test a Relationship

1. If the couple will not move apart after several sessions of our urging them to do so, we suggest: "You could continue living under the same roof but sleep in separate bedrooms and discontinue having sex. But this discipline is so difficult, we suggest it only as a fallback option."

2. See chapter 9, particularly pages 153–156.

3. For a brief overview of these myths as well as some concise answers, see chapter 1, pages 5–6.

4. Rudy and Faith Buettner, with Mike and Harriet McManus, *Marriage Savers Mentors' Guide: Using the FOCCUS Premarital Inventory*, rev. ed. (Potomac, Md.: Marriage Savers, 2007). See the special section on how to help cohabiting couples, pages 61–72, plus Exercises 18 and 19, pages 110–14.

5. Blaine Fowers, "Predicting Marital Success and Divorce Using PREPARE," a summary of a study published by PREPARE/ENRICH (master's thesis, University of Minnesota, 1983).

6. FOCCUS is an acronym for Facilitating Open Couple Communication Understanding and Study. For more information, contact FOCCUS, Inc., Family Life Office, 3214 North 60th St., Omaha, Neb. 68104, (402) 551-9003 or toll free (877) 883-5422, www.foccusinc.com.

7. PREPARE is an acronym for Premarital Personal and Relationship Evaluation. For more information, contact Life Innovations, P.O. Box 190, Minneapolis, Minn. 55440–0190, (651) 635-0511, www.lifeinnovations.com.

8. Do not leave the decision to take an inventory up to the couple. It should be required. When we proposed making it optional one semester, no one wanted to take it.

9. Recordings of Dr. Knecht's talks can be ordered from Fourth Presbyterian Church, 5500 River Road, Bethesda, Md. 20816, (310) 320-3600.

Chapter 8: Mentors and Mentoring

1. Buettners with McManuses, *Mentors' Guide*. Marriage Savers has also produced a secular version of the guide to help nonreligious couples build marital skills. A third edition is geared toward parents or expectant parents

who are unwed. Its goal is to increase the quality of the couple's relationship so that they might consider marriage. The exercises are designed to be administered by social workers in a welfare (TANF) agency or Head Start if a couple is not religiously active, or by Mentor Couples if they are in a church. We recommend using the abridged edition of FOCCUS with such couples.

2. Yet it is not unusual for peer-based ministries. In Alcoholics Anonymous, for example, a million Americans attend AA meetings weekly. In metropolitan Washington, D.C., 1,800 AA groups meet each week, with typically thirty to fifty people attending. That's 72,000 people who are mentoring one another. Yet only a tenth of Americans are alcoholics. Half of new marriages are failing. Thus, the potential for marriage mentoring is enormous.

3. W. K. Halford, H. J. Markman, G. H. Kline, and S. M. Stanley, "Best Practice in Couple Relationship Education," *Journal of Marital & Family Therapy*, 29(3), 2003.

4. The Barna Group, "Christians Are More Likely to Experience Divorce Than Are Non-Christians," *The Barna Update*, December 21, 1999.

5. Training Mentor Couples should be an ongoing process, since over time couples will move away, retire, withdraw from the program or for other reasons.

6. As lay people, mentors are trained never to advise a couple if they should marry. However, professionals such as a pastor or a therapist have the authority to be more candid.

7. Of course, if a church demands six months of marriage preparation, it will lose many couples to less-demanding churches. That serves no one well—neither the demanding congregation nor the couple, nor the other church. That's why Marriage Savers has persuaded clergy in more than two hundred cities to adopt a Community Marriage Policy, in which virtually all pastors in a community agree to require four to six months of marriage preparation. The result is that the divorce rates for entire metropolitan areas such as Austin and El Paso have been slashed in half! See chapter 10 for details.

8. In fact, we ask each mentoree to sign a Mentoring Consent Form, in which they absolve the mentors and the church from responsibility: "We acknowledge and understand that we take full responsibility for the decisions

made by us regarding our relationship and do not hold our Mentor Couple or the church liable in any way for those decisions." The couple signs three copies: one to keep themselves and one each for the church and the mentors. We have never faced a lawsuit involving inventories or mentoring.

9. B. J. Fowers and D. H. Olson, "Predicting Marital Success with PREPARE: A Predictive Validity Study," *Journal of Marital and Family Therapy* 12, no. 4 (1986): 403–13.

10. For the complete study, see Latimer and McManus, "How to Give Marriage Insurance."

11. Michael J. McManus, *A Manual to Create a Marriage Savers Congregation,* rev. ed. (Potomac, Md.: Marriage Savers, Inc., 2003). This is a 183-page guide on how to launch five major marriage reforms in any church: preparation, enrichment, restoration of troubled marriages, reconciliation of separated couples, and stepfamily assistance. It contains a detailed appendix with brochures, evaluation forms, and other material that can be adapted for any church.

12. Meyers is the cocreator of an excellent premarital inventory, Zoë. What is unique about it is that the research behind every item on the inventory is made available to its users, whether clergy, a Mentor Couple, or premarital couple. Zoë can be taken online. For more information, call Rev. Meyers at (913) 345-9700. As of July 2006, two thousand churches were using Zoë.

13. Jeffrey Meyers, "A Pastor's View of Mentoring," in McManus, *A Manual to Create a Marriage Savers Congregation,* 59–61.

CHAPTER 9: TEACHING RELATIONSHIP SKILLS
HECTOR AND TERESA: A CASE STUDY IN MENTORING

1. Buettners with McManuses, *Mentors' Guide,* 6.

2. After a few years of offering rigorous marriage preparation, more and more couples coming for marriage preparation had no connection to our church but were urged by their friends to come for the mentoring.

3. See Howard Markman, Susan Blumberg, and Scott Stanley, *Fighting for Your Marriage* (San Francisco: Jossey-Bass Publishers, 1994).

4. One characteristic of cohabiting couples is that each partner lim-

its his or her investment of effort and time to 50 percent. One puts the garbage in the trash can, and the other carries it out. But neither wants to do the 51 percent and put a new bag in. They prize *independence* rather than *interdependence.*

5. See chapter 3, ". . . and Abused (The High Risk of Violence Among Cohabitors)."

6. One of the saddest elements of cohabitation is that it erases the traditional lines between being single and being married. An engagement has always been a high point of a young woman's life. For cohabitors, however, the wedding day and honeymoon have lost much of their luster because the couple is already living together.

Chapter 10: The Community Marriage Policy

1. Community Marriage Policy® and Community Marriage Covenant® are Marriage Savers trademarks.

2. *10 Great Dates* DVDs and a paperback book can be ordered for $50 per set from Marriage Savers by calling (301) 469-5873.

3. REFOCCUS and *A Manual for Extended Use* can be ordered from FOCCUS, Inc., (402) 551-9003.

4. Marriage Savers trains "back-from-the-brink" couples to save marriages in a Restoration Marriage Ministry based on the McGinnis model. For more information, call (301) 469-5873.

5. Diane Sollee, former associate director of the American Association for Marriage and Family Therapy and now director of Smart Marriages in Washington, D.C., cites several academic studies with evidence that fewer than one fifth of couples seeking help from therapists find that help.

6. *Reconciling God's Way* workbook, *Hope for Your Marriage,* and *Harmony for Your Home,* Joe and Michelle Williams, International Center for Reconciling God's Way, Modesto, Calif., 1997, rev. 2006. This can be ordered from Marriage Savers by calling (301) 469-5873.

7. The Williamses' powerful personal testimony can be found in their book *Yes, Your Marriage Can Be Saved.*

8. According to Dr. E. Mavis Hetherington, University of Virginia, in a phone interview.

9. *Creating a Successful Stepfamily Ministry,* by Rev. Dick Dunn, is a kit that includes a manual, a CD that the organizing committee listens to, and a paperback book, *Willing to Try Again.* The kit can be ordered from Marriage Savers at www.marriagesavers.org.

10. National Council of the Churches of Christ in the U.S.A., *Yearbook of American and Canadian Churches* 2007, ed. Eileen W. Lindner (Nashville: Abingdon Press, 2007).

11. This is not the case with Catholic churches, where the average Catholic priest is dealing with 1,500 to 2,500 people—ten times the membership of the average Protestant church. And Catholics have a "common marriage policy" in all parishes that requires six to twelve months of marriage preparation from the time a couple meets with the priest until the wedding.

12. Paul James Birch, Stan E. Weed, and Joseph Olsen, "Assessing the Impact of Community Marriage Policies on County Divorce Rates," *Family Relations* 53, no. 5 (October 2004). (See this article at www.marriage savers.org.)

13. For example, in 2006 the small town of Morris, Illinois, in rural Grundy County, had a divorce rate of 82 percent. Neighboring LaSalle and Bureau counties had divorce rates of 79 percent and 62 percent, respectively. For 2002–2005 the tri-county divorce average rate was 81 percent.

14. From remarks tape-recorded at the Family Research Center by AP Radio.

Made in the USA
Lexington, KY
21 February 2018